ADVANCE PRAISE

It is clear from page one of the book that Leo knows the AEC business extremely well. He tells story after story of specific cases where a problem was faced or issue identified, each time with some solid advice and suggestions for what one can do in a similar situation. Super easy to read and entertaining on every page—and I say that as someone who doesn't like most management books!

MARK C. ZWEIG
FOUNDER AND CHAIRMAN, ZWEIG GROUP

The perfect leadership user manual to help think through the challenges, stay true to your values, balance a million competing demands, and grow into a successful team builder and leader.

TOVA PELTZ
REGION PROJECT DELIVERY MANAGER,
OREGON DEPARTMENT OF TRANSPORTATION

From the Ground Up covers a topic that is seldom addressed in higher education or in the professional workplace. An excellent resource for those looking to demystify transitioning from "doer" to leader in the AEC industry.

RICH MITCHELL
AIA, NCARB, GGF, ADJUNCT FACULTY, NEW SCHOOL OF
ARCHITECTURE AND DESIGN

Leo provides relatable real-life stories, self-reflection exercises, and proven practical skills and tools that serve as a compass and inspiration for readers to lead themselves in charting their course to reaching their goals.

MIKE BAKER
VICE PRESIDENT, DAVID EVANS AND ASSOCIATES

Essential reading for aspiring A/E/C firm leaders! Balancing billable work with the demands of strategic and operational responsibilities is not for the faint of heart. Leo MacLeod provides a roadmap with real-world examples and practical strategies to achieving success as a doer-leader.

ALLISON TIVNON
AUTHOR OF *MARKETING AT LOW TIDE: HOW TO RECESSION-PROOF YOUR MARKETING DEPARTMENT*

The steps in this book are the same ones I followed when Leo coached me as a new leader. He encouraged me to be honest with myself, to acknowledge what I need to be successful, and to feel confident putting my needs first.

REBECCA GRANT
PRINCIPAL, IBI GROUP

The textbook for project managers who want to grow as leaders. Fun and easy to read.

ANDREW FORT
DIRECTOR, EDUCATION PROGRAMS AMERICAN COUNCIL OF ENGINEERING COMPANIES (ACEC)

from the ground up

STORIES AND LESSONS FROM ARCHITECTS AND ENGINEERS WHO LEARNED TO BE LEADERS

Leo MacLeod

Pie House Publishing

Pie House Publishing
7045 SW Ventura Drive
Tigard, OR 97223
www.leomacleod.com

Ordering Information
For details, contact leo@leomacleod.com

Hardcover ISBN: 979-8-9856822-0-5
Paperback ISBN: 979-8-9856822-1-2
eBook ISBN: 979-8-9856822-2-9

Library of Congress Control Number: 2022905340

Printed in the United States of America

First Edition

For Grace

ACKNOWLEDGMENTS

I am so grateful for all the people who contributed their ideas, energy, and talents to the making of this book: Susan Williams, Todd Sattersten (and his support group of other business book writers), Jerry Keefe, Dan Hess, Mike Baker, Rich Mitchell, Izzy Sigrest, Allison Tivnon, Jerry Yudelson, Terry Krause, Alison Hoagland, Rebecca Grant, Amy Friendy, Josh Lighthipe, Kris Carlson, Kent Larson, Gerry Langeler, Brad Hermanson, Mark Zweig, Tova Peltz, and Mark Poe. Special thanks to my editor Kristin Thiel, who patiently listened to me while I grappled with the writing process and always left me laughing. When I've needed it the most, it was my wife, Lisa, who gave me the support and encouragement to put one foot in front of the other to finish. I love you.

CONTENTS

Introduction: Juggling Chainsaws xi

STEP 1: CHART YOUR COURSE 1
Lead Yourself 3
Know What You Want 11
Understand What Your Firm Needs. 19
Learn How To Get There. 25
Get What You Need 33

STEP 2: DON'T TRAVEL ALONE 41
Get Support 43
Invest In Relationships. 53
Do What You Say. 65

STEP 3: CONSERVE ENERGY 71
The DIS Multi-Tool: Introduction 73
Delegate What You Can. 77
   Know What To Shed. 77
   Own Your New Role 85
   Consciously Communicate 89
   Push It Back 97
   Ask Great Questions 105
   Accept The Acceptable 111
Ignore The Unimportant. 117
   Know What's Important 117
   Know What To Ignore 125
   Ignore Distractions. 135
   Don't Ignore Planning 141
Shrink To What Works. 147
   Take Small Steps 147
   Count Small Wins 153
   Shrink To Fit. 159
   Get It Done. 165

STEP 4: THE VIEW FROM HERE 169
No More Chainsaws 171
Surprise Yourself. 179

Notes 181
About The Author. 185
Field Notes 187
One Final Note. 189

INTRODUCTION: JUGGLING CHAINSAWS

Pete is a successful project manager at a hundred-person architectural firm in St. Louis. He's always dreamed of being an architect, but now, nine years into his career, he's at a crossroads.

Liz, one of the firm's partners, approached him with a once-in-a-lifetime opportunity to run the fast-growing senior housing division. It would mean managing thirty-five people—a big jump from the seven he manages now—as well as being responsible for overall profitability of the sector. It's a big bump in pay and prestige. He would be one step closer to being named a principal. From there, he could become a partner. Owning a firm is everything he and his wife have worked for. But it's not a done deal.

Liz was clear with Pete that she is confident in his abilities but thinks he will have some challenges making the transition from doer to leader. She wouldn't be talking with him if he wasn't an excellent individual contributor: talented at designing and managing profitable projects, successful at building client loyalty and repeat work, and well-liked by his staff and peers for his integrity and easy-going attitude.

But there's more to managing a department than successfully managing his own projects. Can he continue to do his projects, make his clients happy, and lift his head up to see what's going on and needed in the firm as a whole? Can he make decisions and advocate for people not on his projects? Can he work collaboratively to create a vision for where his department might grow relative to the market and competition? Can he switch his focus from project management to routinely monitor the staff utilization rates to make sure people are billing as much as they can? Can he be direct and assertive at times when people are underperforming? Does he know when to be quiet and use diplomacy to make sure people don't get upset and leave? Can he hire and mentor the right people to make sure they are successful? Liz raises valid questions. Pete has his own doubts if he can make the transition from doer to leader. He doesn't know if he can let go of control of some projects and let others do the work that's given so much personal satisfaction. He doesn't know if he has the temperament and abilities to work with people who might not share his commitment to accuracy and taking care of clients. He's not sure he can think outside his projects to focus on the organization.

His biggest concern is having enough time in the day to do it all. This promotion will mean more hours, not less. He already feels exhausted trying to meet the demands of everyone:

- **His supervisor,** who is watching how well he's using his team
- **Clients,** who want his undivided attention
- **Direct reports,** who want seemingly constant direction and attention
- **His wife,** who would like an empathetic ear at the end of the day (not to see how fast he can fix her problems)
- **His buddy,** who just wants him to return his text about the invitation to go hunting this weekend
- **His kids,** who want ten minutes of kicking the soccer ball in the backyard (not to watch TV with him. . . while he checks his email on his phone)

As Liz talked about the promotion, Pete started to calculate the additional people he will need to please: colleagues in other departments; owners of the firm; new talent who will need to be recruited and coached.

He already feels like he's juggling chainsaws: so many important things are in the air that he feels like if he misses and screws up, bad things will happen. With the promotion, he'll have more responsibilities and the need to reach even higher standards, but Pete will have less control, in some ways, since he won't be doing much of the work anymore. As one leader I have worked with put it: "You need time to innovate and plan for what we can't see and make sure things don't break while you're not looking."

If Pete isn't up for the challenge, Liz will need to look elsewhere for another candidate. That stings, in no small part because how could he report to anyone else when the opportunity was his to seize? But is it worth it? If it's going to work, he must fully commit to change.

The Promise

Pete is typical of the emerging leader I've coached for over two decades. Dependable. Ambitious. Overwhelmed. Conflicted. *From The Ground Up* is a practical, well-tested, step-by-step guide to making good use of that drive and managing the turmoil, to understanding what it means to be a leader, not just a doer, in the architecture/engineering/construction (AEC) industry. In this book are the same fundamentals of the highly successful leadership program I developed for American Council of Engineering Companies (ACEC). It's a process that has proven to work for thousands of emerging leaders who had the same questions Pete faced and who discovered a leadership path to a rewarding career and a meaningful personal life.

You'll find a lot of value in this book no matter what industry you're in. I've shared this same playbook with project managers in high-tech, financial services, and the public sector, for instance. But if you're an architect, engineer, or construction project manager, this book is written especially for you. In other industries where doers are trying to switch to leading, the path is less cluttered. But in the design and construction industry, the path to ownership is trickier to navigate. Being an AEC leader is more akin to having your own business: not only are you ultimately responsible for the work but you also have to find and train new people, manage them, bring in new clients to sustain it all, and, somewhere in there, find time for administrative work, billing, infrastructure, and strategic decisions.

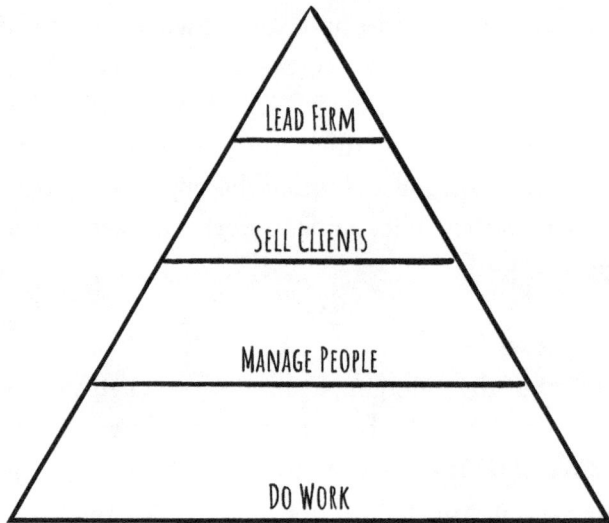

```
            /\
           /  \
          / LEAD FIRM \
         /------------\
        /  SELL CLIENTS  \
       /------------------\
      /    MANAGE PEOPLE    \
     /----------------------\
    /         DO WORK          \
   /----------------------------\
```

Yes, you get compensated more as you move up, but there's more at stake and more to balance. The risks and pressure to balance grow. At most firms, even leaders at the top worry about how much of their time is billable. While you're taking time in the boardroom to identify the vision of the company, there's still an expectation you'll find time for doing project work, managing others, and contributing to business development. You don't get to drop responsibilities. You're just adding more to your plate. Unless you develop some strategies for working smarter, you'll be like our friend Pete, looking up at the ceiling and wondering what the point is.

The book is organized in terms of a journey, beginning with your goal and giving you solid strategies to get to your destination, starting from where you are today.

- The first step, **Chart Your Course**, is designing a vision that is unique to you. Having a life, pursuing your passions, and playing a significant role is a custom, one-off design job. No one else can be the author of your plan for yourself. I start out by helping you design a destination that marries what you want, what others want from you, and what skills you need to develop to get there. When you create a vision for yourself, you'll be taking the first step in becoming a leader: leading yourself.
- The second step, **Don't Travel Alone**, is understanding that leadership is about the relationships you build. Every interaction at work or at home informs what kind of leader people see when they look at you. It's not a solo adventure but a lifelong pursuit to grow and nurture your relationships. I introduce you to the concept of the emotional bank account to help you identify where you're making the right step and where you're off course and hurting your progress.
- The third step, **Conserve Energy**, is learning how to conserve energy, keep commitments, and build your team's capabilities with a simple formula: DIS, which stands for *delegate* what you can, *ignore* the unimportant, and *shrink* to what works. By learning how to be more conscious and intentional about what you're doing, you'll work smarter, get more done, and have energy to devote to what's personally important.
- The fourth step, **The View from Here**, is seeing how the strategies in the book come together in a new way to help you balance competing priorities and enjoy the ride!

Each chapter starts with a story of an emerging leader, their challenges, what they learned, and what next step you might consider in the journey. At the end of each chapter, there are exercises and challenges you can do by yourself or as part of a team. The organizations that have gotten the most value from these strategies have internalized them, talked about them, and made them part of their culture, always asking questions of themselves such as: *Are you making a deposit or a withdrawal? Is that task the best use of your time? Were you clear in communicating why your colleague needs to own their part of a project?*

Whether you have three years of experience or thirty years of experience, this book can help you make the transition to a new level within the organization and bring you more aligned with what's important to you personally. Let me be clear: it is a transition. You need to accept that the habits that have made you successful as a doer can actually keep you from becoming a successful leader.

What got you here isn't going to get you there.

To get there—the place where you are respected as a professional, influence others to do their best work, and maintain sanity—you'll need to adopt a new sense of your role beyond being a doer. To be acutely aware of how you're spending your time and what you're focusing on at any one time during the day. To reevaluate how you approach projects, how to play a strategic role, and how to mentor others so they're not feeling overmanaged. Recognize how much you talk, what you say, and when to say it.

Perhaps the most fundamental shift will be to set boundaries and tell yourself and others no, rather than saying yes to everything: sitting through another pointless meeting that goes over time; listening to a long-winded explanation from a colleague when you're running late; accepting another project when you've already upset current clients by not meeting timelines; using your lunch hour to prepare for an interview for a project you have no chance of getting; working late to catch up on emails again. I'll show you the art of controlling your own schedule rather than being held hostage to all the demands on your time. *From The Ground Up* will be your emergency aid kit to help you navigate it all and keep moving forward.

You can skim the book and then put it away somewhere. Or you can dig in and do the work. There's no shortcut to the top. All that matters is how much you want to get there. I've been blown away by the people who really worked the strategies in this book, and how quickly they saw results:

- The working mom who cried one week after feeling like a failure and who smiled the next week, after learning how to reduce meetings from twelve hours a week to two hours
- The engineer who didn't understand how to let go of work but grew to be the single best person at delegating in a 200-person firm
- The senior architect who enjoyed being the smartest person in the room but transformed into a respected leader who found making others shine was more rewarding

You are in charge of your future. You can create your own path. I'm going to show you how.

STEP 1

chart your course

3 Lead Yourself

11 Know What You Want

19 Understand What Your Firm Needs

25 Learn How To Get There

33 Get What You Need

LEAD YOURSELF

A leader is one who knows the way, goes the way, and shows the way.

JOHN MAXWELL

Nora was a managing director of landscaping for a prominent integrated design firm when I met her. She felt pulled in many directions from the partners, each having a different idea of how she should spend her time: pursue international projects that will elevate the firm profile, pursue local projects the firm can win, focus on managing the team, focus on specific partner projects, increase billable time, and spend more time networking and making connections.

If she followed one partner's advice, another partner was upset she wasn't following their priorities. Nora didn't like to disappoint people, and yet, that was all she seemed to be doing. She found herself repeating, "Sorry," and hustling to address the next hot issue of the day. Her influence with the partners and her team was weak because she lacked focus and purpose. She wasn't being a leader; she was simply following others. She wasn't a person with a strong vision of what she wanted to accomplish.

The only person she wasn't considering on a regular basis was herself. And that was what was really weighing on her. Understanding that she was clearly unhappy and frustrated by the lack of clarity from others, I asked her to put herself first for a change:

What does life look like three years from now?

She looked at me, thunderstruck, and said, "That's a good question." All she had been able to think about up to this point was what was needed of her—a critical component of success that can't be ignored. But I wanted Nora to start designing her future with what she wanted for herself.

Emerging leaders show their leadership potential by putting the needs of others before themselves. They don't want to be difficult. They don't want to let people down. They don't say no. They are always at service to what others want—clients, colleagues, and their managers. But dedicating all your energy to serving the company to the exclusion of serving your personal goals isn't sustainable. You end up as a team player and a yes person without a sense of personal direction or conviction. Companies tend to demand as much of you as you're willing to give. If you're always putting the company first, other parts of your life can pay the costs. Your personal satisfaction of what you work on can suffer. Your health can suffer. Your peace of mind can suffer. Your personal relationships can suffer. And when these suffer, your perception as a competent leader suffers. You can continue to be an excellent individual contributor, but your ability to influence others suffers.

It's up to you as a leader to plant the flag and say, here's what's important, based on your own assessment of what's important. Leaders don't look for direction; they create it and get people on board to make it a reality. Your vision of being a successful leader is a combination of three parts: *what you want*, *what your firm wants*, and *how you will get there*. In the next three chapters, I break this out so you can design your own vision, but first, back to Nora.

What Nora Wanted

In an ideal world, landscape design in Nora's firm would be respected as a legitimate discipline. As it was, only some partners understood that landscape design was not a last-minute complement to a project, but part of the design. That it integrated the built world into the natural world. That the orientation, scale, shape, and materials of the building took into consideration the actual site of the building. That her team would be introduced to the client right from the beginning as an integral part of the team. The voice of the landscape designer would be heard and respected.

What Nora wanted was to focus on the kinds of projects she dreamed of working on in college: exciting, transformative designs that you see on the covers of industry magazines. The kinds of projects where schedule and budget are not the only priorities. The kinds of projects that make money for the firm as well as elevate the firm's status and reputation.

Nora also wanted a life outside the office. She was a prisoner of her phone, always checking, day and night, for work messages and responding right away. She didn't have good boundaries over her time, so she'd skip dinner because she was working late; she accepted requests for endless meetings that drained her day; she was too tired to work out at the gym, even though she knew it was exactly what she needed. She was not averse to putting in the time, but she wanted to unplug too. Maybe even get back into dating!

So how would Nora describe her ideal world in three years?

"First of all, I'd have an awesome boyfriend who liked to hike and explore nature with me. Bonus points if he likes to garden and cook! I'd actually get back into the gym on a regular basis and lose some pounds. I'd like to feel like I'm defined by more than just work. Professionally, it would be amazing to be taken seriously at my firm and listened to. I don't have illusions that I'll win over everybody, but if I had one to two projects that excited me and my team, it would be easier to do the boring, last-minute planting plans. I would be taking the time to travel and learn from other designers so I could expand my perspective. I need more than just me designing projects so I can dedicate more time to winning work, marketing what we're doing, and managing the team."

What Her Firm Needed

The partners agreed on one thing: To grow, and to attract and retain good people, they needed high-profile, more-profitable projects. But the firm traditionally made its money on commercial and industrial projects where landscape design, and design in general, was minimal. There was a palpable tension between "this is where we've made our money" and "this is where we want to make our money." It was an ongoing debate without resolution: What if we turn down this work and focus on higher-profile work that will win us awards? Will we alienate our core clients if we become known for higher design—read, higher-fee—projects? Should we stay focused on taking care of our core clients and not try to be someone else? Or is that a dead-end strategy that won't attract new talent and keep us from growing?

How to Get There, Together

What Nora wanted to do and what the firm needed were not totally aligned, but Nora started to see an opportunity to meet somewhere in the middle. She thought long and hard about her interests and the reality and eventually defined a three-year vision that had *enough* of her passion and skills but also reflected the needs of *enough* partners for her to be ultimately successful.

She identified a handful of influential partners who really wanted higher margins and higher-visibility projects where landscaping wasn't an afterthought, the kinds of projects that would appear on the cover of *Architectural Design* and make the architects look good, a goal that worked for both her needs and the firm's needs.

There were people who weren't on board with her direction, and for them, she and her team would still need to draw up boring plans, but enough of the right people supported her once she was able to articulate her vision to them in terms of why it made sense to the firm. Her critics also became quieter when she started to win projects attractive for every role at the firm. While she had to compromise and do some things she didn't like or wasn't good at, she did enough of what she liked and was good at bringing it all together.

Missing Skills

Nora understood there were two areas she needed to develop: relationships and time management. Her desires and needs weren't going to be met if she didn't understand how to finesse her relationships with key people. Understanding how to read a room, digging into the psychology of what motivates different people, was a higher-level relationship skill that she didn't need when she was just managing projects. She needed to study people, think about her approach, and rehearse how she was going to present her case.

In terms of time management, she understood that her biggest obstacle was herself. She was bad at letting go of control. Like Pete back in the introduction, she didn't say no, took on too much, and ended up disappointing people. As her coach, I shared the time management and relationship skills I cover later in this book to help her stay focused, set respectful boundaries, and choose times to say no.

Nora tucked fifteen minutes into her day to watch TEDTalk presentations related to her job and ambitions and jot down her own thoughts for case studies. Too much of Nora's time was being consumed by managing the schedules of her team's projects. She found someone who was better at details and organization to take over those responsibilities so she could focus on other things. Nora sat down with the person and was clear about her goals to elevate the department and empowered the staffer to push back when Nora wasn't delegating effectively and taking projects back. We rehearsed difficult conversations with key people to help assert her position and understand what others need.

Putting It Together

Two years after she and I worked together, Nora was at the podium at the national conference for Urban Land Institute in Chicago, presenting one of her projects to 300 people. Later that evening at a cocktail reception, the CEO of a competing firm asked what it would take for Nora to move to Los Angeles and join his firm. When Nora returned from the Chicago trip, the partners asked to convene a special meeting on Friday to talk with her about her vision for the department and how they could support it. She would love to, she said, but she had a previous engagement (a picnic with her new boyfriend) and asked her assistant to schedule a meeting with the partners as soon as possible.

⭘ What Nora Learned

1. Understand the common company goals that are supported by the greatest number of people.

2. Engage allies who can champion your case and involve them in model projects.

3. Work with everyone and don't make enemies.

4. Enlist the help of your team by sharing your vision and how they can help.

5. Build the skills necessary to get to your destination.

Nora's plan checked a lot of boxes: She started to engage people in bigger ideas, apply her plan to the current project, and market that project to a national audience to gain more attention for more prestigious and profitable work for the company and work that was more exciting for her too. She delegated responsibilities to people who were more talented in those areas, in addition to taking time to improve the organization and relationship skills she needed.

Nora found success at her firm by being keenly aware of the politics and power dynamics among the partners. She understood it was essential to have the support of enough important partners to elevate landscape to a serious discipline within the firm.

She also knew that some partners weren't supportive of her, for reasons she may never comprehend. Nora needed to tread lightly in her transition to leadership by making sure she didn't make enemies with partners who could determine her future. She needed to take care of their needs, listen to them, and be perceived not as a threat to their own agendas.

Nora also learned that being a leader means not having people love you all the time. It's being confident and smart about your choices. Willing to defend your decisions. Knowing that while compromise is necessary to make things happen, you can't ignore your own interests. Nora needed to make herself a priority, as does any emerging leader. As she became more successful articulating the case for integrating landscape into the project design, she also became more successful impressing on clients, partners, and employees that her personal passion was integral to the organization's plans. People started to take notice. When a young designer on her team confided in Nora that she was his role model, Nora realized the impact of her influence on others. She began to understand that her real value to the organization was not about her work as a designer but about her influence as a leader. And most importantly, she became willing, and able, to lead herself.

Put Yourself in the Path

Aligning your dreams with reality is a tricky business: aim too high and you almost certainly risk being let down by life; aim too low and you can feel like you've given up on what could be, even before you start.

Nora couldn't control many things in her life, but she put herself in the path of things going favorably by following a plan. She adjusted her goals to the reality before her by looking at what could be. Nora didn't limit herself and give up by accepting that things would never change. She took action, and it paid off. Leaders don't stay in one place, but instead, they "skate to where the puck is going, not where it has been," said the hockey great

Wayne Gretsky. Think of your vision as where you want your puck to go and where the company's puck may be heading too. Nora found success by heading in a common path and staying open to what opportunities could arise.

In the next three chapters, I help you do the same. First, as I did for Nora, by introducing you to the concept of your mountain by clearly identifying your interests and passions. Second, by looking at your firm's needs to align your mountain and their mountain. Last, I help you identify the skills and tools you'll need to put it all together.

○ **Try It**

Journal on these three questions:

1. **How much of your life is in service to your company?**

2. **In what ways are you seen as a follower?**

3. **In what ways are you seen as a leader?**

KNOW WHAT YOU WANT

The secret of getting ahead is getting started.

MARK TWAIN

The key to Nora's happy story is that she started with a plan that put her needs first. She didn't just accept that other people had her best interests in mind. She didn't trust that doing what others told her to do was going to make her happy. Nora learned that when she invested the time to think about her own needs and interests, it gave her a bearing for her own unique course. Taking the time to think about what she wanted helped fuel her journey and motivated her when travel became difficult. The energy and passion that kept her engaged and focused on the path also helped shape her perception as a strong leader, someone to follow.

To become a leader who helps set a vision for your organization, you need to first learn how to set a vision for yourself. To make your tough journey worthwhile, ask why you are doing this.

What's at the end that's worth the extra work?

The Mountain

A few years ago, driving up to Mount Hood to ski, I saw a hitchhiker with a snowboard on the side of the road. I hitchhiked across the country in 1977 from New York to Oregon. These days you don't see many hitchhikers, but this young woman could have passed for one of my kid's friends. Beth was twenty and full of the kind of stories that were like my own—raised in a small town; college didn't feel right to her; struck out on her own; working any job to get by. She didn't have a direction for her life until one day as she was serving chili and pie in a Shari's restaurant, she looked out the big plate glass window at Mount Hood. "It was as if the mountain was calling to me," she said. "I didn't know how I was going to get there, but I just put one foot in front of the other." The morning I met her, Beth was on her way up to her job as a housekeeper at a resort on the mountain so she could spend the afternoon snowboarding and the night partying. She had found and conquered her mountain. It wasn't the destination that impressed me about her story but the simple formula that she was able to fix her sights on a not-so-distant goal, intentionally move toward it, and eventually get there.

When I look back on my career path, I see it traced a similar haphazard route. Instead of being illuminated by a grand vision for how my life would work out, I just followed my curiosity and took steps in any direction that seemed right to me at the time. One thing led to another: from housepainter to freelance writer to college student to fundraiser to advertising executive to consultant to coach. I have a career and life I never would have dreamed of as the teenager who tried to project himself twenty years down the road. It turns out it was too far to see. Like mountains in the near distance, smaller life goals are also easier to identify and conquer.

The metaphor of moving toward a mountain can be useful in helping you create a plan for your future. You may not know where you're going in five or ten years. What work you'll be doing. If you'll be at the same firm. Be in a committed relationship. Still live in the area. Or even if you want to be an owner someday. But when you ask someone where they might be in three years personally and professionally—as I did Nora—it's an easier question to answer. One year goes by too quickly. Five years seems too far away to imagine. But three years is a better time frame to visualize how life will be different from today and allows more time to pace yourself to accomplish anything of much significance.

Design Your Mountain

To define what's important to you as an emerging leader, take a few moments and think about what life would look like three years from now. What's important to you, what you would like to achieve, and how you want to be spending your time. Ask yourself:

What does life look like three years from now?

Live and Work

Start by defining your personal goals so you don't design a plan without considering what's in it for you. Create a plan around just your career goals and you may find yourself leading two separate lives, one at work and one at play.

This is a time to focus on what will make you happy and fulfilled, not what others want or expect of you. To stay engaged and motivated to make it to your mountain, your personal goals need to be part of your plan. Ask yourself:

- *What do I like to do in my spare time that I'd like to do more of? Golf? Time with my kids?*
- *What do I want to make sure to do before time runs out? Travel to Japan? Build my own house?*
- *What are my relationship goals? Settle down? Have kids? More time with family? More time with my partner?*
- *What are my personal goals? Do I want to lose weight? Get stronger? Be less anxious? Run a marathon? Play the banjo? Learn Italian? Be less judgmental? Laugh more?*
- *Is community important to me? Do I want to be more involved in my neighborhood association? Volunteer to help the those in need?*
- *Is spirituality important to me? Do I need to find a community of like-minded people? Develop a practice?*

- *Do I want to set limits on how much I work? Vacation time? Spend a month in Tuscany? Scuba dive the Great Blue Hole in Belize?*

Without carrots in front of us, we can stay too focused on our careers and miss the living that goes with life. I show you how to manage your time more effectively so that these are not just items on your list but things you check off as done.

PASSION

Ask Why

Project managers, designers, and engineers in the building industry are fortunate to see the product of their work every day in schools, office buildings, industrial parks, streets, and bridges. But too often, they lose the why behind their work in the busyness of doing the work. They lose the connection and meaning to their work.

When you're sitting in your chair with your paper and pad, reflect on why you do what you do. Simon Sinek in *The Power of*

Why claims, "Very few people or companies can clearly articulate **why** they do **what** they do. By **why** I mean your purpose, cause or belief." Asking yourself the **why** behind your goals can help you see the larger view at the top of your mountain. Continue to ask yourself *why* behind your mountain to uncover the larger truths.

- *Why did I get into this career in the first place?*
- *Why does my company exist?*
- *Why do I get out of bed every morning?*
- *Why would a larger role help me lead a fuller life?*
- *Why would it help others?*
- *Why would it help the community?*
- *Why should anyone care?*

Matt, who leads a heavy civil contracting firm, fell in love with paving the roads that take people from home to work, to soccer practice, to the brewery to meet friends, to the next state for vacation with family. The work he does connects people with each other to build and maintain relationships. Roads mean businesses can grow, which brings prosperity to everyone. His work connects people in many ways to build stronger communities. Matt sees his work every day as he drives on the highways he paved. He doesn't lose sight of why he puts in the hard work.

If you define your mountain in terms of your passion and pursue responsibilities that excite you, you'll bring more energy and commitment to all your work—even the stuff you don't like. With a blueprint of what's important, you'll orient yourself to actively seek opportunities that engage you and make you feel like you are contributing to something larger than receiving a paycheck. Your mountain brings together everything that's important to you and has meaning into one frame.

Get Down to Business

After reflecting on your passion, it's time to ground it in reality. Try to put yourself into the future in terms of how you'll be spending your time and how you'll be engaged in projects. Visualizing by putting yourself actively in the future will help you shape a picture that's beyond words and really helps you see your mountain. In three years from now. . .

- *How will my day be broken down by percent of time devoted to certain tasks and responsibilities?*
- *How have I set specific metrics to reduce time on technical tasks that others can easily do?*
- *Do I have a different title with larger responsibilities?*
- *What kinds of projects are rewarding?*
- *What clients are great to work with?*
- *What initiatives in the office am I spearheading?*
- *How does the culture of the office reflect my contributions?*
- *How do I show leadership in my industry?*
- *Are there specific awards, speaking engagements, or forms of recognition that help me mark success?*

The more specific and quantifiable you can be in defining your mountain, the sharper in focus it will appear, and the easier it will be to get excited to move toward it. Here are some examples of mountains.

Be an assistant department head. *Spend 35 percent of my time in business development and resource planning for future projects (compared to 10 percent now). Actively mentor younger designers by knowing the needs of my team and finding opportunities for them to grow each day. Build a strong alliance with other assistant department heads so we meet regularly and support each other. Improve in financial management and be able to track profitability more consistently. Learn to let go of work and relax. Establish a regular practice of meditation. Go to a meditation retreat in Novia Scotia for a week.*

Move into an owner role within my company. Reduce my project workload by 40 percent. Help the owner make strategic decisions for the company's growth. Grow the company to seventy-five people—sustainably. Play a primary role in screening and hiring people. Be a better listener and learn to read body language. Establish stronger boundaries around time and have a much better handle on focusing on highest and best use of time. Plan one major family vacation each year. Take a Friday afternoon off each month to hang with my son. Go to Hawaii with my wife—alone.

Be a recognized expert in energy modeling. Present at a Greenbuild conference. Produce five net zero buildings. Delegate most of my old work and hire and train the right people. Spend more on business development and growing a network. Have a hard stop at 5:30 to be home for dinner four nights out of five. Go on an annual fishing trip with my son on Deschutes River.

If you're moving through life and making decisions with your mountain in front of you, you'll have greater success than if you let life happen to you, as Nora discovered. You'll be the author of your life instead of a supporting actor in other people's plays. You don't have control over getting a promotion, but you can influence the outcome. You could be let go tomorrow, or you could move into a larger role. You may not even know if your current company is the place for you to be, but give it your best guess.

An emerging leader once asked me, what if the mountain you're going toward isn't the right mountain? And then he caught himself and answered his own question, "Maybe there's another mountain behind it." Exactly. Who knows what will happen or what you will discover on your three-year journey toward your mountain. One thing is certain: you won't find out by sitting and thinking about it. It doesn't matter how small of a step you make or how long it takes. What matters is continually making progress through action, even if it's imperfect action—a misstep, a dead end, bruises along the way.

Recall that while Nora put together a plan that put her needs first, it was tempered by what her company needed. You can't disregard the interests and needs of the stakeholders who can either help or derail your progress. In the next chapter, we look more closely at how to adjust your dreams to your current reality.

○ Try It

1. Block out an hour when you'll be uninterrupted to reflect and in a clear mind. Suggestion: not at your desk with people around you and not when you're drained at the end of a tough day.

2. Write the word *Why* and jot down thoughts on why you do what you do and the difference it makes in the world. Enlist the help of a colleague or friend to help generate thoughts.

3. Ask yourself this question: *What does life look like three years from now?*

4. Draft whatever is in your heart. Don't be critical or get caught up in wording or if it's possible. Be as specific and tangible as possible in describing your future life. Use action verbs to describe the action you need to take. List any specific accomplishments or outcomes, including any changes in mindset, behavior, attitude, or how you're spending your time.

UNDERSTAND WHAT
YOUR FIRM NEEDS

Mountaintops inspire leaders but valleys mature them.

WINSTON CHURCHILL

Nora's successful strategy was based on the reality that enough of the partners were supportive of her dreams. Her vision mirrored the vision of the company to get bigger, more exciting projects. As she moved forward, she continued to make the case for her vision not in terms of what she wanted but in terms of what was in it for them. Nora wouldn't have been successful if her personal vision and the company vision didn't share a common intersection. The art of becoming a leader is mediating what you want with what other people want, landing in the sweet spot between what you want to do (passion) and what the firm and market are willing to pay for (need).

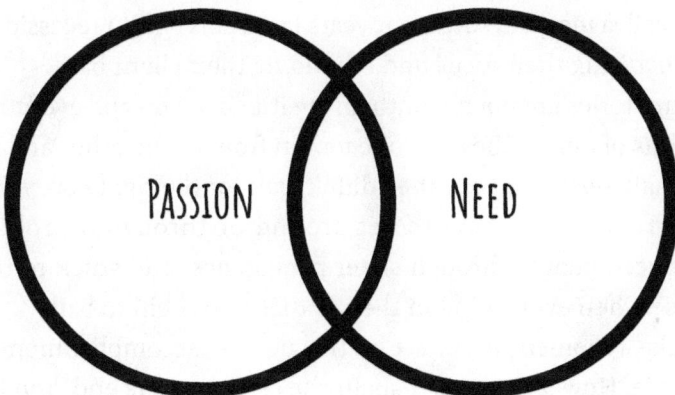

PASSION   NEED

In a perfect world, Nora's vision for her career would have aligned perfectly with what the firm wanted from her. But as her story illustrates, the real world is not always so friendly to our dreams. Nora's real success was in navigating the challenges that she faced and staying focused on her own goals in the process. At times, she had to do work that was not aligned with her dreams. The other partners had different priorities. She was thrown off course by a demanding client who insisted she work on his project, rather than having her staff handle the work. Illnesses, vacations, and changing support staff all, at different times, made it necessary for her to temporarily put her goals on hold.

The leadership course is a constant process of starting down your path, getting delayed or pushed off course, and resetting your compass and getting back on course. It doesn't stop. Set your direction. Move forward. Hit a roadblock. Go through it or around it. Move forward. It requires a keen sense of direction to stay on course for what you want and take care of other people too.

The Gift of Struggle

When I ask seasoned AEC leaders what accomplishments they are proudest of, the stories are always about overcoming big obstacles: managing scary, high-risk projects sooner than they thought they were ready; royally screwing up and being publicly chastised by a client, only to turn the project and client around; getting laid off from a firm and starting their own; being embroiled in a lawsuit with colleagues and settling it years later; surviving a recession by restructuring their focus and rebuilding their client base.

The stories are not about them creating a vision and everything going as planned. They put one foot in front of the other and met the challenges head on. They didn't wait for the right conditions. They figured out how to get around or through a problem, convinced people through sheer persistence, and stuck to their course when everything in their bodies told them to bail.

Take a moment to reflect on the greatest accomplishments in your life. How much was it about the reward at the end, and how much was it about the discovery of what you're capable of doing? At this moment, you may be wondering if it's worth it, if you have the right stuff. But if you think back on what you are proudest of, weren't there moments of doubt and wanting to give up? Sure, but they didn't stop you. Although you couldn't see it at the time, those obstacles served as monuments to what you are capable of overcoming. Without them in your way, you would never have experienced the deep satisfaction that comes with the trial and work of testing your resolve, strength, and resiliency.

Strength and resilience are not qualities we're born with. We learn them while adapting to challenging experiences:

- Calming ourselves as a baby after a few good nights of loud crying teaches us to take care of ourselves when others aren't there.
- Diving back into dating and making ourselves vulnerable after our heart has been broken teaches us that we can trust again.
- Saying yes to a new work challenge and sweating over how to do it teaches us how self-reliant we can be.
- Working through a pandemic and adjusting to stay focused and productive teaches us that we can adapt to change and things outside of our comfort level, perhaps more than we imagined.

When we're in the middle of the struggle, we may want to give up. But we go on despite how hard it is, and that effort of going through the steps—despite our feelings—is what builds the muscle for being more resilient.

Even when we're faced with a difficulty, we may not be immediately buoyed by the knowledge that we've gone through this before, that we can do it. But we get stronger over time, and it becomes self-evident that we can take comfort in our strength and resilience. We learn to rely on our strength to overcome obstacles.

When we don't know what to do and feel overwhelmed by forces outside of our control, we can remember there have been other times when this was true—and we survived. We can get through it, and we'll be stronger and more resilient for the next challenge. We'll be proud of what we can accomplish.

What's in It for Them

Look through the lens of the leaders of your firm to fully understand the company's mountain, or three-year vision. The emerging leaders I've worked with who have risen the fastest in their careers thought and acted like owners already. They spent time asking questions and taking an interest in how the company operated and learned about their short- and long-term goals. When they were made principals, it wasn't because they had future promise as leaders. They had already demonstrated their leadership with their actions. The promotion wasn't a promissory note but a recognition of what they already did: acted with other people in mind, questioned what was good for the whole of the organization, advocated and supported people outside of their team. If you're serious about moving up, start thinking like an owner. Be curious and ask senior leadership questions like:

- *What are the strategic goals of the company?*
- *What markets or clients are expected to grow, shrink, or remain the same?*
- *What does the firm need to evolve to be more competitive with others?*
- *What are the most talked about subjects at the board level?*
- *What positions do you see yourselves hiring for in the next year?*
- *What economic or market shifts are happening or are on the horizon?*
- *How are customers behaving differently in how they're doing business that might affect your company?*
- *What skills will be needed in the staff?*

- *How can I best help you summit your mountain?*
- *What are the hot buttons of the most influential stakeholders?*

Your mountain represents your future three years from now. But it's more realistic to achieve your goals if you operate within what ownership is looking for in the next three years. You'll enjoy more support for your agenda if you've framed it in terms of what's in the best interest of the firm. It may require modifying your mountain to what's realistic and scaling back some expectations. It may mean adjusting your timeline out to five years, instead of three.

Becoming an owner is an action with purpose not a title without meaning. It's a verb not a noun. Start acting like a leader today and take into account the company needs.

◯ Try It

1. Ask senior management questions about the direction of your company to learn what's on their minds.

2. Talk with colleagues and do research online to forecast how your industry may be changing in the next five to ten years.

3. Invest in joining an industry association for your profession, such as the American Institute of Architects (AIA), American Council of Engineering Companies (ACEC), or Associated General Contractors (AGC) to educate yourself about trends.

4. Share your ideas with people you trust. Articulating your vision moves it from an idea in your head to something closer to real. This can be particularly powerful if you share it with a spouse or partner, as it can bring you closer to sharing your dreams and working as a team to support each other.

5. Share it with your supervisor to understand how achievable your vision is and gain an ally who can help advocate for you. Leave it alone and come back to it every quarter. It takes more than one sitting to fully compose a vision. Thoughts and ideas will come to you as questions start to arise. You'll look at senior leaders differently. You'll start to make note of what you don't want to see.

LEARN HOW TO GET THERE

Before you are a leader, success is all about growing yourself.

JACK WELCH

Once Nora knew where she wanted to go, it became clear that what got her here wasn't going to get her there. Up to this point, her focus was on executing great design. She needed better time management skills to shift her focus from projects to organizational concerns. She needed to find time to have those important conversations and build strategic relationships. Sure, some of her day was spent on interpersonal issues with staff and partners, but if she wanted to increase her influence with both of those groups, she knew she needed to be a better communicator and read people better. She still needed to be focused on projects, but she needed to be more focused on people to reach her goals and elevate her department. She alone wasn't going to get this job done. She needed to build trust and collaboration with people at every level of the organization.

IQ and EQ

Researchers Jack Zenger and Joseph Folkman asked more than 300,000 business leaders to rank the top four competencies from a list of sixteen key leadership skills. The team then ranked the data from most important to least important skills that leaders need to succeed in their current positions.

COMMUNICATES POWERFULLY AND PROLIFICALLY
COLLABORATION AND TEAMWORK
ESTABLISHES STRETCH GOALS
SOLVES PROBLEMS AND ANALYZES ISSUES
INSPIRES AND MOTIVATES OTHERS
DISPLAYS HIGH INTEGRITY AND HONESTY
CHAMPIONS CHANGE
PRACTICES SELF-DEVELOPMENT
DEVELOPERS OTHERS
BUILDS RELATIONSHIPS
TAKES INITIATIVE
DEVELOPS STRATEGIC PERSPECTIVE
INNOVATES
CONNECTS THE GROUP TO THE OUTSIDE WORLD
DRIVES FOR RESULTS
TECHNICAL OR PROFESSIONAL EXPERTISE

0   10   20   30   40   50   60   70   80

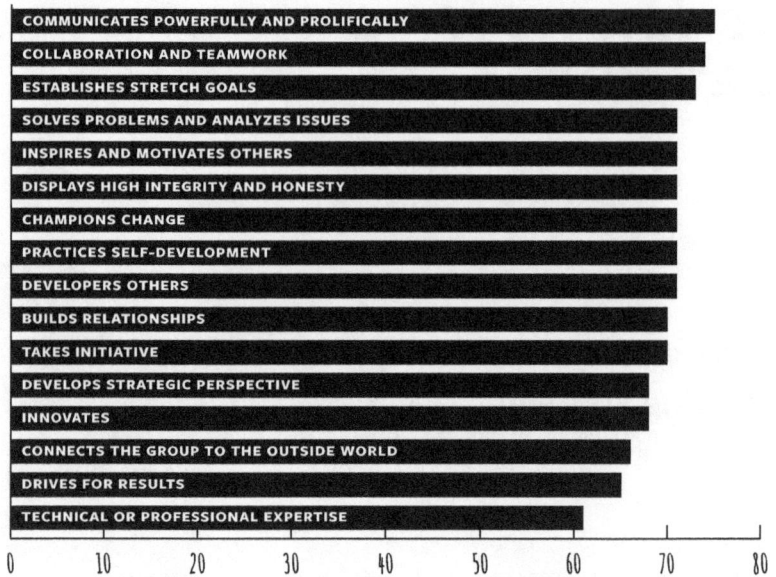

The study showed what we intuitively know: technical skills, while important, don't differentiate the most effective leaders. The soft skills of communication, essential to managing people and influencing others, rated the highest.

I decided to conduct my own survey of the AEC industry. When I interviewed one hundred AEC business owners about their biggest leadership challenges, their number one issue was not finding better technical experts but finding people who can relate and communicate with peers and clients. Not to engineer something or solve a technical problem. But to be aware of what's going on with their own emotions, to manage their emotions, to read people, and to have the sense of how to talk to someone. To know when to listen and be empathetic like a therapist. To know when to be direct and as clear as a drill sergeant. And to know how to do it well so you don't tick people off but gain their admiration and trust.

Let's face it—we want the smartest people in the room when it's engineering the bridges we drive over, designing the schools children attend, and building the high-rises that tower forty stories above the sidewalks. For executing complex tasks, we value precision and logic. We want those people to be sticklers for details. We want them to take ownership of their work. We want them to always do the right thing and be accountable to the highest standards. Technical experts with high IQ are indispensable to any AEC firm.

But when it comes to delivering bad news, resolving interpersonal issues, motivating other people to perform at their best, and convincing an interview panel to hire you, math is not the most useful skill. Technical skills are undeniably important to solving technical problems. But to solve people's problems, you need a different skill set.

"Engineers need the full skill set of hard and soft skills to be effective leaders in the AEC industry," says Alison Davis, executive director, ACEC Oregon. IQ is the common predictor of intellect, but it doesn't help gauge soft skills, which is equally important. Emotional intelligence, or EQ, is our ability to understand and manage the emotions of ourselves and other people to have better interpersonal relationships. Author Travis Bradberry notes, "EQ is so critical to success that it accounts for 58 percent of performance in all types of jobs."

It's not that IQ and technical skills are irrelevant. They do matter, as psychologist Daniel Goleman explains, but they are the entry-level requirements for executive positions. Goleman, who first introduced emotional intelligence in a 1995 book by the same name, says, "Emotional intelligence is the sine qua non of leadership. Without it, a person can have the best training in the world, an incisive, analytical mind, and an endless supply of smart ideas, but he still won't make a great leader."

To get a personalized assessment of your EQ, pick up a copy Bradberry's book, with Jean Graves, *Emotional Intelligence 2.0*. The book breaks EQ into four buckets: self-awareness of your thoughts, emotions, triggers, and behavior; self-management of your thoughts, emotions, and behaviors; social awareness of other people's cues, emotions, and perspectives; and relationship management, which leverages a total understanding of yourself and others to have more successful, productive relationships. Bradberry provides quick and easy strategies to boost your EQ.

Nora learned how to be aware of her perception as a leader, how often she said yes, how difficult it was to let go of work, and how she communicated verbally and nonverbally to the partners. That required self-awareness. She needed to take the time in her day to plan her priorities, communicate clearly with her team so they could do the work without leaning on her, and bite her tongue when a partner was chastising her at a meeting. That required self-management. Nora learned to read the room and know when to speak and when to be quiet, to listen closely to truly understand what was important to someone else, and to spot those times when a staff member really didn't understand a task but was afraid to say anything. That required social awareness. She learned when to say yes and when to say no, when to push and when to sit back, how to gain support by making others feel important, and how to communicate so people listened. That required relationship management. EQ is a skill that can be developed over time. You can learn how to listen, communicate, and think strategically.

New Tools

In the design and construction industry, leadership starts from the ground up. You need to master both the technical skills to lead projects and the soft skills to get the best from people. Look honestly at what's missing from your tool kit and dedicate time to improve your skills.

What skills and knowledge do you need to get to your mountain?

As a doer now, you can think about what technical skills will be critical to instilling trust in others that you are competent for the bigger project challenges? If your mountain is to focus on more

PASSION NEED

SKILLS

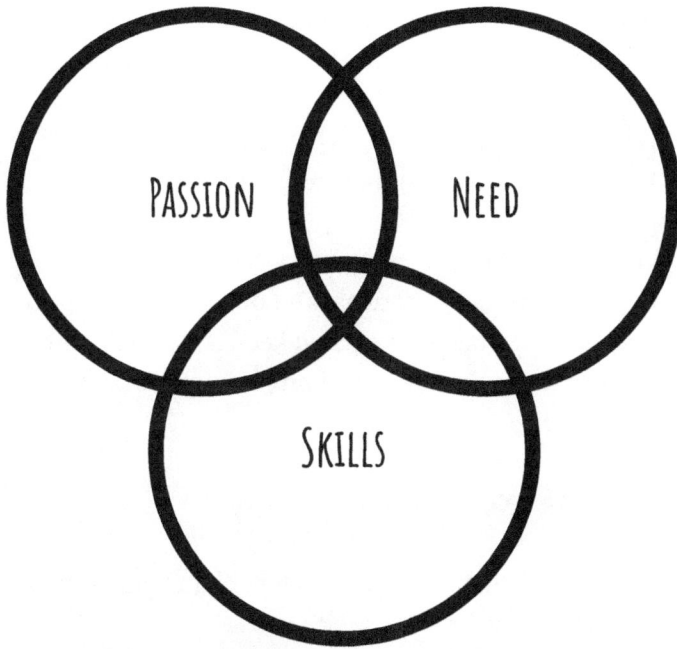

complex projects or take on a larger role, what might be missing from your toolbox?

- Learning how to estimate and bid on projects
- Mastering design software
- Producing financial projections
- Understanding how to assess and manage project risks
- Doing more public projects
- Designing a LEED Zero school project
- Mastering the art of group facilitation
- Learning how to design and lead effective meetings
- Getting your license

Following is a sample of skills in my leadership readiness assessment (the end of this chapter has more resources). Review the skills most called for in AEC leaders to understand how you rate on a scale of 1 (weak) to 5 (strong):

INTERPERSONAL COMMUNICATION

- Engage people easily and take the time to connect with them
- Listen to and understand what's being said
- Have strong self-awareness and impact on others

TIME MANAGEMENT

- Organize the day effectively and budget time for priorities
- Manage meetings actively and keep discussion on track
- Balance managing tasks and projects with interacting with others

PEOPLE MANAGEMENT

- Delegate tasks clearly and effectively
- Coach staff to provide options for solving problems and keeping the project on track
- Give constructive feedback in real time

CONFLICT RESOLUTION

- Take responsibility for resolving issues in a timely manner
- Wait until calming down before addressing conflicts
- Think through the issues and consider everyone's perspective

DECISION-MAKING

- Are adept at navigating change where there is no clear answer or method for proceeding
- Take initiative instead of looking for direction
- Think strategically about the growth of the organization

BUSINESS DEVELOPMENT

- Present themselves persuasively to win work
- Build strong, long-lasting business relationships
- Understand the psychology of why clients select firms

LEADERSHIP DEVELOPMENT

- Are candid about personal shortcomings and seek input to grow
- Develop better peer relationships and learn how to support each other
- Build a strong network of peers for guidance and support

Some firms are better at providing training and professional development than others. There's more than one way to build skills, which can include a combination of:

- Self-study online or outside reading
- Personality assessments to understand your strengths and weaknesses
- Formal training and certifications
- Mentorships
- Project opportunities to gain exposure or build competency
- Observing people who model the behavior you admire

If you want a good idea of what skills to develop, turn to the people who currently hold the positions you desire. Better yet, talk to them for advice on what they suggest. What were their experiences when they were starting out? Since they know you, what areas would they suggest you develop? Building skills and knowledge is not one of the "when I find time" activities. Weave skill building and getting smarter into your day, as you're making your way.

○ Try It

1. Make a list of technical skills you'll need.

2. Identify soft skills; download my assessment at www.leomacleod.com.

3. Ask your supervisor for feedback on your performance and what they think you need to do to grow. Taking the initiative and being open to receiving feedback is a strong move to your mountain. It signals your intention that you're serious and committed to the work of becoming a leader.

4. Send them your list, revised to incorporate their notes.

5. Map out a specific plan for what you need to focus on in the next quarter and how you'll develop your skills.

GET WHAT YOU NEED

It is a rough road that leads to the heights of greatness.

LUCIUS ANNAEUS SENECA

When I met him, Amir was a twenty-two-year-old engineer who designed airport transportation systems. Very bright, personable, and responsible, he was on the leadership track at his 300-person consulting firm. He was well compensated, and he liked the company culture and his supervisor. But the workload and pressure to meet deadlines were relentless. Amir was frustrated that he didn't have time to develop the skills that would help him grow. The lack of mentorship made him question whether this was the right firm for his goal, or mountain, of being named associate in three years. Maybe another firm would be more supportive of his dreams and help him get there? When Amir posed the question if he should look elsewhere, I said I didn't know, but in the meantime, I asked him:

How can you start moving toward your mountain today?

Maybe a move to another company was best. But while he was figuring it out, he could also start moving toward his mountain at his current firm and not wait for ideal conditions. He knew the skills he needed to work on. How could he find ways at his current firm to strengthen his skills? He didn't need a formal mentorship to focus on listening and communication skills, for instance. While he wanted someone to sit down with him and show him how something works, what could he learn from observing other people, asking a quick question on a technical issue from time to time, reading a book, watching YouTube videos, and attending webinars? A lot. He took my advice and started to look for creative ways of getting what he needed.

That was five years ago. Amir is still at the same firm and is a senior associate. He realized he was able to accomplish his mountain at his current company. Making the best of what's in front of you, adapting to the realities before you, is a skill you will continue to need and develop as you ascend.

○ What Amir Learned

1. **There's a lot you can do to get what you need.**
2. **No situation is ideal, but you can learn to adapt.**
3. **Your resourcefulness will help elevate your perception as a promising leader.**

Start Today

Amir could go somewhere else, but every company has its challenges. The moment you make that move—whether it's to another firm or working for yourself—you're likely to discover a different roadblock you didn't see coming. Conditions for moving toward your mountain are never perfect.

Amir will be that much further down the road in his development as a leader if he does later switch companies. But he will also discover, as Nora did, that you can often get what you need where you are if you are creative and persistent. If he does want to grow his leadership, how will his supervisor see his leadership potential if he is constantly complaining about not having a mentor?

Dave Lakey, who has held several executive positions, suggests there are two kinds of employees who each elicit a collective sigh of relief. Let's say it's a typical meeting. One person enters, and the group sighs, thinking, *Whew, everything's going to be OK because they are here and will help us reach a decision/solution.* The other kind of sigh of relief is when a different person leaves the meeting, and the group thinks, *Thank goodness! That person was taking us nowhere. Now the rest of us can get to work!* The first kind of employee is an Oh Yes employee, and the other is an Oh No employee. Even though Amir is well regarded at his firm, complaining about what he isn't getting could easily get him labeled him as the Oh No employee instead of the Oh Yes employee. His stock as an emerging leader could be compromised if he can't demonstrate resourcefulness and creativity to solve his problem.

His chances of influencing his supervisor to promote him are much greater if he shows initiative and resourcefulness to develop himself without help. His supervisor may want to support him, but they also want to see him doing everything he can to solve his own problems. What's more, Amir may prove to himself he has more control and power than he imagined. He isn't waiting for things to happen or for optimal conditions; he is taking control over his future, and that mindset will serve him, wherever he goes. "Don't think that you don't have control over your future just because you work for a firm. Seek out and say yes to work that you want to do more of," says Mike Baker, VP, David Evans and Associates.

Nora's challenge was less about finding resources to grow and more about getting buy-in for her mountain. Amir's challenge was less about resistance to his plans and more about not getting the resources to grow. Whatever the challenge, it still comes down to an obstacle to face and navigate through or around. You won't get everything you want. No one does. Your growth as a leader will be in how well you adapt to that reality. How can you get your needs met, meet the needs of the firm, and build your skills in your current environment?

When Do You Decide Something Is Just Not a Good Fit?

There are two instances in which more effort doesn't pay off: gaining and sustaining skills of being a leader are too much of a stretch for you, and/or the company culture is not a place where you can make progress or be happy.

New to the role of being head of IT for an accounting firm, Nguyen struggled with the transition from help desk to management. On the one hand, those above him had been so confident in his abilities that they'd just handed him the role, and he also didn't like the idea of reporting to someone else. On the other hand, he really hated dealing with people's problems. He always found a new emergency to occupy his attention rather than navigating a difficult conversation with a colleague. In this position, he felt like he was a square peg in a round hole. Nguyen eventually decided that management wasn't for him, and when he made the decision to step down from his role as head of IT and go back to the help desk, he felt enormous relief. Someone else filled the job of IT director, and they appreciated having Nguyen deal with all the customer emergencies while they troubleshot internal concerns. They each had their strengths and by working together were happier and more productive.

What are your strengths?

Companies often try to promote their smartest technical people into management positions, sometimes with poor results. Aligning mountains is not just the job of emerging leaders. Smart companies align people with their strengths. I have coached a number of emerging leaders for whom the transition was just too much—not for any reason other than some people are better suited to be individual contributors rather than leaders of others. Assessments such as Predictive Index, DiSC, StrengthsFinder, and Myers–Briggs are worth investigating and have their advocates in developing leaders.

If you're not being supported at your firm with your own goals, it may be that the firm has different needs and a specific role for you to play. Is your only option to leave and go elsewhere? Do you just hold out for the right conditions that support your goals?

Do you have the support for your mountain at this firm?

Sisyphus, the king of Ephyra in Greek mythology, was punished by the gods by being forced to roll an immense boulder up a hill only for it to roll down every time it neared the top, and he had to repeat this action for eternity. You may feel like Sisyphus. The reality is that sometimes it is futile, and it's better to look elsewhere. Here are some scenarios I've encountered with clients where more effort wasn't going to pay off:

- A senior leader's mountain is to become an owner, but after ten years, the current ownership does nothing to recognize or reward the effort. The reality is that the existing owners aren't sure they can ever let go, and they need the senior leader to just run projects.
- An environmental engineer who is promised relocation to Alaska to be closer to family is ignored or not taken seriously. The reality is that starting a new office is risky, and the need is greater for the engineer to grow existing clients in their current market.
- An associate architect who wants to develop her own clients is not given any time or opportunity to work on anything other than the clients of the firm's principals. The reality is that the principals have the mindset that taking care of existing clients' every immediate need holds precedence over everything else.
- A project foreman who does everything she can to advance to superintendent is not listened to or respected by her peers and is passed over for a promotion, a less-qualified man getting it. The reality is that the people who

STEP 1: CHART YOUR COURSE   GET WHAT YOU NEED

make the decisions haven't had the opportunity to see her performance and rely on reports from senior project managers, who happen to want to promote their buddies.

It's important to be seen as a resourceful and compliant team player. And when there are obstacles, it's equally important to show you can be strong and resilient and surprise yourself and others. But if you've put in the time and made the effort, it's just as important that you check in with yourself. Is this an environment where I can be successful, based on what I'm seeing? What are the chances that they are going to change, or are these rocks just too big? When your mountain and the company's mountain clearly don't align, revisit what's important to you and have the courage to put yourself first.

Before you take the leap to another firm, take the initiative to sit down with management, and state your needs in no uncertain terms. If you're at the end of your rope, let them know what it will take to keep you. It's not uncommon for people to avoid tough but necessary conversations like this. If you're ready to leave, you don't have anything to lose by being totally honest.

Even if you feel like management is a good fit for you, transitioning from a doer to a leader who also does doer-level work can be draining and lonely. The rest of this book is dedicated to giving you help.

We first look at the power of relationships to help you get to your destination with the support of people and a solid base of support. I then help you reclaim your time, conserve energy, and build your team by delegating and managing all those distractions that get in the way of moving closer to your mountain.

○ Try It

1. On a piece of paper, create two columns. In the first column, list five skills that you need to develop to be a successful leader. In the second column, indicate how you will develop that skill. Example:

   SKILL
   Keep others accountable for results

   HOW
   Be clear up front

2. Find another emerging leader to share your results and discuss strategies.

3. Pick up a copy of StrengthsFinder to help you identify your strengths.

4. Have an honest and open conversation with your supervisor about your questions and concerns.

5. Ask yourself how you can creatively develop one skill in the next week without asking your supervisor for anything.

6. If you feel like your company isn't aligned with your mountain, start trying to identify what their priorities are to at least understand the misalignment.

7. Share your mountain with your supervisor frequently so they understand what's important to keep you engaged and happy.

STEP 2

don't travel alone

43 Get Support

53 Invest In Relationships

65 Do What You Say

GET SUPPORT

Be strong enough to stand alone, smart enough to know when you need help, and brave enough to ask for it.

UNKNOWN

Alison represented the ideal emerging leader: uber-responsible, accountable, ambitious, and always ready to say yes to a new challenge. Popular with clients and staff, she was on a fast track to leadership. An architect and mother of two young children, Alison wanted to become principal in five years and spend more time with her family. An enormous challenge, but she believed anything was possible if she worked hard enough.

Alison had been brought up to believe being a leader meant doing it all by herself. A very competitive person by nature, she compared herself to others. Being successful, she believed, was all about shouldering responsibilities and not asking for help. She felt like she had something to prove and that working harder was the only path.

The construction industry is extremely challenging: tight deadlines, difficult personalities, high risk, and pressure to perform all the time. Alison was responsible for some of the firm's most important, and often the most demanding, clients. When she came home, she had to kick into high gear to give attention to her two young children—and husband, when she could find the time. The challenges were taking a toll on her: "I felt like I was not only letting myself down but everyone who expected so much from me." Constantly stressed and sleep-deprived, Alison withdrew emotionally from family and friends. The demands of doing it all were breaking her down. "I was giving everyone 120 percent. Everyone, that is, except myself," she said.

As her coach, I encouraged her to take time to take care of herself, even though she felt that would be selfish and a sign that she was not strong enough to be a leader. One day, her husband, who had been by her side from the beginning and helped her find balance, forced her to go to the gym. She reluctantly agreed, and something amazing happened. She jumped on a treadmill, and "that literally saved my life. I was on a path to failure, and I wasn't being successful at work or at home. I had let everything get the better of me," she told me.

Her village of support had always been there for her: Her mother and mother-in-law provided childcare, and her husband adjusted his schedule and worked cooperatively to find the right balance at home. But Alison had to be OK with asking for more help and accepting it. Her supervisor could see the strain, and he shared his personal story of discovering how you can't let work drag you down and dominate your life. "What I hadn't realized is that they had been waiting to be asked," she said. Her community wanted to be there for her even more. "That was the turning point. It only made me stronger to accept the help of others."

Alison realized that her tight grip on every aspect of her projects was a barrier not only for her growth but also for the growth of the people on her team. When she began to let go of control and learned to lean on her team, her leadership path changed from a solo to a collective journey. Instead of doing it herself, she found opportunities to let go of responsibility so other people could shine. Consequently, it took the stress off her and, in turn, made the team members feel good about what they were doing.

She started each day by identifying what tasks she could delegate and to whom, taking the time to pair people's strengths with the right tasks. Alison had to learn to be a better listener, take the time to understand her team, make herself available to coach them when they floundered, and give constructive feedback to keep them accountable. Instead of doing all the work, she focused more on supporting her team.

In Alison's new view, a strong leader is successful at home and work. "We're fooling ourselves if we show the world that it's all about careers. The main reason we have a career is to bring joy and life in other areas of our lives. I now find joy and pride in both my career and what I do outside of work." When she mentors young people, many of them women, she is open about what she's learned, both the successes and hard lessons: you don't need to sacrifice a personal life to be successful, don't do it alone, and learn to let others shine. It also requires commitment and hard work. "Young people need to hear that it's often a struggle to be successful. But working through the struggle is where you see the most success and where you really learn about yourself."

⦿ What Alison Learned

1. Get to your mountain faster and easier by asking for and accepting help.

2. People are there to support you: partner, family, supervisor, and team. You need only the humility to ask.

3. Pushing responsibilities down to your team is not wrong; in fact, it is a gift and opportunity for them to grow.

4. If you want to be there for other people and bring your best work, you need to make yourself.

Alison ended up becoming principal in three years, two years short of her goal. She and her husband bought a tent trailer to do more family vacations, and she found a used banjo on Craigslist and is learning her first bluegrass song.

Successful leaders learn the hard way you don't achieve success by going solo. You need allies to make the journey possible and to juggle all those chainsaws. Balancing the demands of doing your job, taking on new responsibilities, and trying to change habits that have worked for you in the past can be exhausting and draining. The mantle of responsibility can weigh on you like an eighty-pound pack.

If you want to climb the highest peak in the world, you can't do it alone. Edmund Hill might have been the first person to get credited for scaling Mount Everest in 1922, but he wasn't alone. A team of people made it possible. Today, if you hired a guide service to take you to the top, you would carry a light backpack, while Sherpas typically carry up to eighty pounds of food, propane, and bottled oxygen. To make it to the top of your mountain, recruiting your team is your first step.

Design Your Team

The team you design for your journey will be unique to your situation and needs. Here are some people I think are important to have in your corner.

YOUR SUPERVISOR

When I coach people to define their mountain, I encourage them to first share their mountain with the one person directly tied to their success: their supervisor. Think of this person as your guide. The person who can take you from here to there along the quickest path. They are responsible for your workload and focus. If they know where you are headed, they can help you get there. Oddly, few emerging leaders take this step, which is too bad. How can the person most directly tied to your success help you if you haven't shared your plans with them?

Is there a danger you'll come across as too pushy and ambitious? All the supervisors I've worked with would rather have the problem of someone with ambition and a plan than someone without a plan and always asking for direction. As mountains rarely align perfectly with reality, your supervisor most likely had similar challenges fitting their own mountain into the demands of the job. They can relate to where you are and can help.

Smart supervisors will not be threatened by your dreams. Instead, they'll work with you to shape the demands of the job with what drives your life and career goals, as Alison's supervisor did. If they know you want to become an associate principal in two years, they can tell you what you need to get there. They can put you on interview teams and give you coaching to confidently present to prospective clients. They can test you with larger projects and have you manage small teams. As you evolve as a leader, you'll be doing the same thing for people on your team.

YOUR TEAM

Emerging leaders are often most loyal and protective of their team. Layoffs in the firm? *Don't look at cutting any of my people.* Underperformers who need to be talked to? *Hey, you don't know how hard we're working here.* Because emerging leaders tend to be protective of their team, they are also hesitant to ask for their support in getting to their mountain. It feels selfish to them, as they can see everyone is working hard to ask to take on extra responsibilities.

Alison learned that the team often is just waiting to be asked. Everyone is an emerging leader with their own mountains. The only way for people to evolve in their careers is to stretch outside their comfort level, build their competencies, and take on more responsibilities. You can model this by talking to them about your own journey and how you are trying to change your approach to work. Leaning on your team to take on more responsibility makes them stronger and more independent. Don't leave your team behind. Bring your team on your journey.

YOUR CLIENTS

Emerging leaders often feel that the people they are letting down the most as they transition to leadership are their clients. The more they delegate, the less they are directly involved in the work that clients have come to expect from them. Clients no longer get them all the time. They have to work with somebody else.

Leadership transition is not unique to you and your firm. It's likely that your clients are faced with the same challenge: pulling good people out of direct service to grow the company and give opportunities to others. Shifting roles is a natural evolution in organizations. Help your clients understand your position. They may not like it, but they'll understand leadership progression is about giving other people a chance to grow. It's not selfish or irresponsible on your part; it's the right thing to let go of the daily handholding for clients. It's not like you're going away. Your role is still client satisfaction, but you don't need to be involved in the daily details as much. As engineering leader Mike Baker argues, "It's easy to let ourselves believe our clients need us too much to leave them and transition from doer to leader. Our best clients, who can and often do become friends, will support our journey to grow and trust us to find good people to continue the service delivery under our watchful eye."

MENTORS

Mentors are people who can show you the way, either by sharing knowledge or giving it to you straight when you might be going off course.

These guides can be senior leaders who have gone down your path. Some firms intentionally try to set up mentor relationships between senior and junior staff. The mentor and mentee might meet quarterly to review goals, but relationships formed under these conditions rarely stick. You'll find greater success tapping the experience of others on your own if you know what you need and expand your view of how to get it.

To identify how a mentor can help, go back to your gaps in skills and experience. Do you need to understand how to negotiate large, multi-phase projects with jurisdictions? Do you need help giving people feedback? Do you need someone to make an introduction to develop your network? Or do you need someone who can listen to your frustrations and reassure you you're not looking at things wrong? Take some time to reflect and journal on what kind of support you need: help with technical competencies, help with understanding people, and help with navigating career decisions.

It's terrific if you can find one mentor, someone who can meet regularly with you and hold their role as teacher with enthusiasm and purpose. Respect that these people are using their valuable time for your benefit. Make the most of it. Show up, be engaged, listen, use what you can, keep them posted on your progress. Don't see it as a one-way relationship. Make it worth their time. Abraham Lincoln said, "I'm a success today because I had a friend who believed in me, and I didn't have the heart to let him down."

It's just as valuable and more common to have a multitude of mentors who can teach you task-based skills. Amir, in "Chart Your Course," sought the teachings of others whenever and however he could. He didn't seek a formal arrangement. He looked for organic opportunities to learn as he went toward his mountain. If you know what holes in your skills and knowledge you need to fill, stay open throughout each day to catch five or ten minutes here and there. Ask questions of the smart people who know how things work: the BIM specialist, the controller, and the receptionist. Remember that these people may have reserved natures or at least, may not be expecting your enthusiasm. Learn about them a little bit and approach them where they are.

In addition to finding mentors who can teach us, we also need people who don't have a problem speaking up and counseling us when they see us return to old habits or make a move that's not well thought out. These are often colleagues who can gently suggest a change of course. They might remind us that we're talking over people in meetings and that we need to listen more. They might see us slipping into taking on work that junior staff should do and ask if that's a good move. They might read our strongly worded email to a client and suggest picking up the phone instead to avoid any misunderstanding. Guides who are truth-tellers can be the most important people on your team, as they help you build your emotional intelligence by increasing your awareness of your behavior and the impact on others. They have a great seat to view how you're doing on your way to your mountain.

OPTIMISTS

Optimists know how to lift you up when you get down or tired. They're your friends cheering you on as you struggle to finish a marathon. Your mother who always believes in you and can't see how you can't do anything but succeed. Your colleague who helps you shake off losing a big pursuit: "You did the best you could. You'll have another chance soon enough. Let's go get a beer!" An optimist is like a dog in the park: nothing gets them down and every day is a gift. Don't we love those people?

Optimists are important to have on your team because they are in short supply. It's more common to find people who complain and see only what's wrong. They can bring us down rather than up. Surround yourself, instead, with people who set goals, get things done, and see an open road rather than barricades. We draft on their success. They draft on our success. And together, we're better and continue with more energy and resolve.

Mahatma Gandhi said be the change you want to see in the world. If you want more optimism, be more optimistic in your outlook and share your optimism with everyone around you. Be known as that person who inspires and motivates others. As a coach, I try to fill that role as optimist. I'm always looking for any signs of progress, even if it's incremental. Because I'm not immersed in working with people all the time, I have the vantage point of gauging progress periodically: "I remember when we started working together, and look how far you've come. Just keep it up. Imagine where you'll be at this rate in another six months!" Think about the key relationships you have and seek out more of the half-full optimists who see the bright side in everything. Get a coach or at least collect some optimists who will remind you of your awesomeness. It works!

Leadership is nothing without people behind you, but as I discuss next, relationships need to be mutually beneficial to be healthy and strong.

○ Try It

1. **Talk to your supervisor** about your mountain so they can help get you there.

2. **Talk to your team** about your goals as it relates to the firm's mountain so they can help support it. Get to know their mountain so you can help them get there, at the same time.

3. **Talk with your clients** about your shifting role, the importance of their satisfaction, and how your new role can provide more value.

4. **Identify what you need.** List the skills you need to develop to get to your mountain. Spend time defining the kind of work you want to do. Your allies should be people who help.

5. **Identify three key allies.** It's not critical that you designate a person for each role. It's more important that you are mindful that you need support and that you identify the people who can help you achieve your goals. Jot down why these people are important to our journey.

6. **Hang out with optimists.** Take stock in the people who are part of your inner circle. Do they bring you up or down? Do you feel energized after talking with them or ready to give up? Collect more optimists to keep you charged, positive, and moving forward.

INVEST IN RELATIONSHIPS

I've learned that people will forget what you said, people will forget what you did, but people will never forget how you made them feel.

MAYA ANGELOU

Jay is a project manager at a forty million dollar commercial general contractor and part of a team of emerging leaders I was asked to develop. The president of the company said Jay has problems meeting deadlines and being responsive to emails and phone calls. He's always running late for meetings. It doesn't look good and is hurting his prospects for advancement. The president is concerned that as Jay manages more people, he's just setting a poor example for new hires. Could I help him? he wondered. When I meet with Jay, I ask him to relay a typical day.

Jay's day starts at 3:00 a.m. as he lies in bed, mentally bouncing between all he must do. He finally falls back to sleep for an hour until the alarm goes off at 6:30 a.m. His wife nudges him and reminds him it's his turn to take the kids to school, which he hasn't remembered. He's trying to figure out how to get them to school and not be late for a scheduled client meeting that he's already postponed twice, when his wife calls out that the dog peed on the carpet again. Cleaning up gross things is one of his understood marital responsibilities that he's accepted. He cleans it up, skips breakfast, and yells at the kids to hurry because he's late. He doesn't kiss his wife good-bye, silently fuming about the dog and kid transport that are his commitments but have derailed his day before it's started.

After dropping off the kids, he texts his client that he's running late and to start without him. He speeds across town, cutting off several cars, and gets to the meeting twenty minutes late, only to realize he doesn't have the latest version of the requested changes to the design. The structural engineer enters the conference room, and he instantly recognizes him as one of the people he cut off in traffic. Gulp. He texts his assistant to email the latest design drawings right away. While he waits for it, and as the meeting continues without him, he texts other people.

When Jay gets into the office, everyone wants a minute with him, but he cuts them off and tells them he doesn't have time. He needs to sit down in front of his computer and focus. He sees that his email inbox has tripled in size in the last hour. He looks at the newest email, about an office softball league, and even though there are pressing emails, he decides to respond to the softball email. It will just take a second, after all. As soon as he replies, another email from someone else about the softball league comes in, teasing him to throw ice packs in his freezer. One of the guys asks if he can get a ride from Jay, but Jay forgets to respond when his assistant approaches his desk. She runs down a list of things to discuss. A text message comes in while she's talking, and he reads it while half-listening to her. Another text message comes in, and another email arrives with a chime.

His day continues like this: being late to meetings, texting during meetings, half-listening to conversations, being impatient during conversations that feel like they go on too long, and not finding time for important tasks that he promised people. He decides to work late and catch up, when he gets a text from his wife that the PTA meeting is tonight. He says he needs to miss it because something important came up, which is not true. It seems like there are more and more instances like this, where he's letting her down. But she doesn't seem to appreciate all the pressure he's under to juggle so much. He comes home and finds a cold dinner, cracks open a beer, opens his laptop, and answers some emails. Jay gets to bed around 11:00 p.m. because he needs to get some sleep before his day starts again at 3:00 a.m.

The Emotional Bank Account

If you were explaining how to make money to a kindergarten, you might say, "Make deposits and avoid withdrawals, and over time, you'll have enough money for a pony." In all our relationships, we silently keep track of positive and negative experiences we have with people. We remember how people make us feel, as Maya Angelou reminded us. The impact of deposits and withdrawals in relationships has been the subject of study by relationship psychologists Drs. John and Julie Gottman.

The Gottmans have spent over four decades on divorce prediction and marital stability. They wanted to see if there were indeed patterns of behavior, or sequences of interactions, that could discriminate between happy and unhappy couples. It turns out that the patterns are directly tied to how we feel about each other, based on whether we have a positive interaction (deposit) or negative interaction (withdrawal) with a person. Compliment someone—deposit. Cut them down—withdrawal. We consciously and unconsciously track our interactions with people as how many deposits and withdrawals they are making.

The Gottmans could predict whether a couple would divorce with an average of over 90 percent accuracy, based on deposits or withdrawals in emotional bank accounts. In a six-year follow-up study of newlywed couples, couples who remained married turned toward their partner's bids for emotional connection 86 percent of the time, while those who divorced averaged 33 percent. The difference between happy and unhappy couples is how they manage their emotional bank account. When the emotional bank account is in the red, or deficit, partners tend to question each other's intentions and feel disconnected or lonely. But when the emotional bank account is in the black, or positive, partners tend to give each other the benefit of the doubt during conflict.

The Gottmans say that to keep your relationship in the positive perspective, you need to continually invest in your relationships, even during conflict. During everyday life, there should be twenty positive interactions to every one negative interaction to maintain a positive balance. Twenty to one! Better get to work.

When I asked Jay how he did in his typical day in terms of deposits and withdrawals, he said, "Not very good." He made some deposits: like cleaning up the dog's mess (except that was more of an obligation, and he negated the positive by not doing it graciously). But most of his day was dominated by one withdrawal after another: forgetting about commitments, ignoring priorities, resenting what he promised to do, and taking it out on people, short-changing the time he gives to people.

Perfect Accounting System

We like and trust each person in our lives based on our collective experiences with them. We remember how they make us feel over time, and we vote with our actions: we call the friend who makes us laugh, and we ditch the one who lectures us on how to lead our life; we refer the contractor who shows up on time and will never use the one who doesn't stand behind his work; we promote the assistant who has a great attitude, and we hope the high-maintenance employee finds another job.

Whether it's at home or at work, our actions and behaviors shape how we are viewed and treated by others. As serial entrepreneur Christine Comaford-Lynch has said, "The universe has a perfect accounting system." Effective leaders are mindful of how they treat everyone around them. They understand that what goes around comes around and that their success is directly tied to the strength of their relationships.

Through our coaching, Jay is starting to recognize the tell-tale signs that things aren't going well: the cold shoulder from his wife for spending more time on his cell phone at home; a frustrated look from colleagues who are routinely cut off or ignored; angry texts late at night from clients who are not getting timely

Building Relationships
1. Make deposits
2. Limit withdrawals
3. Give it time

responses about schedule; complaints from the president directly on how his poor time management and lack of responsiveness will keep him from moving up.

How Jay treats people makes them feel unimportant and not valued. And that's just one day in his life. You can imagine how over time his behavior will be like slow leaks in his bank accounts with everyone. The equity will be drained if he doesn't address making withdrawals.

○ What Jay Learned

1. Treating people poorly, even if it's not intentional, has consequences.

2. Withdrawals count much more than deposits.

3. Little withdrawals compound over time and aren't forgotten.

4. Poor planning drains your own account.

5. Relationships drive success at home and work.

Check Your Balances

When I share Jay's story in leadership workshops, many emerging leaders see more of themselves in Jay than they like to admit. Being inattentive to the needs of other people does not help gain the trust and support of people who can help you make the journey. What's required to be a great leader is to monitor your deposit-to-withdrawal balances with everyone, particularly with clients, staff, and allies.

CLIENTS

If you're a respected, competent project manager, you already implicitly understand the importance of keeping clients happy by making more deposits than withdrawals. You make deposits by being on time, honest, trustworthy, reliable, responsive, fair, helpful, and personable. You avoid making withdrawals of being late, being unreliable, not following up or being unresponsive, lying, hiding problems, being difficult, coming up with problems without solutions, and being negative or combative.

You know your next job depends on how well you execute on this one. At the end of the project, clients take stock of the overall experience. A developer client once told me, "Construction is a messy business. Issues come up and everyone—the client, contractor, architect, consultants—gets dirty. In the end, when you're all done, you ask yourself who do you want to get back in the ditch with again?" A project might even start out great, but if the client has to nag you about that door that still doesn't swing shut, that's what they'll most likely recall the next opportunity to work together. We tend to remember withdrawals more than deposits, and the most recent withdrawal shades our overall impression. Finish strong if you want the next job.

Not all clients value the same things equally. Understand what's important to your client. Do they want an original, bold, inspired design, or do they just want a solution that's proven to work? While one client counts creativity as a deposit, another might consider it a withdrawal. Does the client want the highest LEED certification, or do they want the most economical design? Consider each client's unique perspective on what constitutes a deposit versus a withdrawal.

In addition to remembering the last withdrawal you made on a project, clients also remember the most frequent and the biggest withdrawals. Nickel and dime on change orders, and the client will remember you keep asking for more money, even if the changes were justified and the final budget was within reason.

I once coached an architect who wanted to focus on higher education. He wanted the universities in Southern California to think of him and his firm first when it came to design work. I asked him what was in his way of developing those relationships, and he said, "When I was first starting out, I was too opinionated and vocal. I yelled at a facility manager at one of the big universities in a meeting with consultants and the contractor." He paused and continued, "There are some holes you can never dig yourself out of." The universe has a perfect accounting system. Better to invest in new relationships while not forgetting the lesson he learned, I suggested.

STAFF

Companies known for delivering consistent and memorable customer experiences all follow the simple principle that the best customer service starts and ends with treating your employees like your customers.

In design and construction, it's not uncommon for project managers to focus so much on taking care of client bank accounts that they drain their accounts with colleagues. Ask yourself if any of these things are true about how you interact with staff:

- *I take the time to see what they're doing and ask what support they could use.*
- *I take a personal interest and ask how their weekend was.*
- *If I cancel a meeting with them, I remember to reschedule.*
- *I refrain from complaining or gossiping about them to colleagues.*
- *I patiently listen to them instead of talking at them.*
- *I give clear direction when giving them work.*
- *I don't lose my cool if they disappoint me.*
- *I ask for their input.*

When I ask emerging leaders these questions in a class, there's often an audible silence. People understand the golden rule: treat others the way you want to be treated. But they forget it or find some way of justifying that making deposits with other people—clients and management—supersedes the needs of staff.

But making deposits with staff is an investment that has a multiplier effect. A study published by the Society of Human Resources Management cited respectful treatment of all employees as the leading contributor to job satisfaction. Another study found that 69 percent of employees say they would work harder if they knew they were appreciated. A third study found that your chances of being disengaged are much higher if you are ignored (40 percent) than if your manager primarily focuses on your weaknesses (22 percent). It turns out, even negative feedback is better than nothing. The key point is that staff who feel respected and appreciated are invested in doing their best work, which makes keeping the client happy easy. Everyone wins.

Neglecting staff can cost you in multiple withdrawals. When staff feels ignored or unappreciated, they underperform. Clients are unhappy, so they lose. You have to swoop in and fix their mistakes, which is robbing you of higher value tasks, so you lose. Staff, who are reliable workhorses, become discouraged by low morale, so they lose. Clients leave, and staff leave, so the company loses. It doesn't take much to follow the thread of the impact. The good news is that it also doesn't take much in the form of a deposit to make a big impact. Little, significant actions can count for a lot more than you think.

Brian, a project architect for a 200-member firm, learned the power of making strategic deposits with staff. He was working on a major hotel project, and a developer was his client. In private-sector construction projects, time is money. The sooner a hotel can open, the quicker they can start taking reservations to pay for it all. The sooner a developer can deliver a functional building, the quicker the hotel can start taking reservations. Everyone gets paid when revenue is generated, but up to that point, everything is an expense. Consequently, there's a constant push to make the architect and contractor do more in less time. Work overtime. Double up efforts. Finish quicker.

Brian was well liked by the hotel developer for his can-do-attitude and ability to deliver on projects. Mild-mannered by nature, Brian always came through and did whatever the client wanted. But saying yes all the time to the client meant more work on his already overwhelmed staff. Deposit for client. Withdrawal for staff. Full bank account for client. Dangerously low account for staff, who were drained from the stress of too much work and unreasonable deadlines.

One day, the developer phoned Brian and said they needed to finish the lobby design a week earlier than scheduled. The developer expected a yes, but this time, Brian pushed back, politely. "I'm sorry," he explained, "I know you want this done sooner, but we can't work any faster than we are." The developer surprised Brian by backing off on his demands. Brian had always assumed that he could never say no to the client. But he learned that with enough equity in your account, a small, reasonable debit doesn't adversely affect the relationship.

O What Brian Learned

1. **Deposits with some people can have a much higher return on investment than the withdrawal you make with others.**

2. **People work harder and may even take on extra work after being supported with a deposit.**

3. **If your bank account is full, you can afford to make withdrawals from time to time.**

4. **In the end, if a project completes on time and the client is happy, small withdrawals during the project aren't significant.**

What Brian hadn't calculated was how the small withdrawal with the client was seen as a big deposit by his staff. When he told his team they didn't have to work the weekend to meet the new schedule, you would have thought they won the lottery. They were so happy and relieved that they could have hoisted him up like the conquering hero and paraded him down the hallway. In the scheme of things, it wasn't a huge deposit, but it was symbolic because Brian was saying, "I understand and appreciate how hard you work. I have your back." That small but significant gesture wasn't soon forgotten, even when Monday rolled around with new demands to speed up the schedule.

Typically, we say yes to clients, and then we make this decision our team's problem. Avoid making a withdrawal with your team by at least talking with them before committing to the client. You might need to shrink the scope of what your client is asking you to do, based on what your team has said that they can do. Once you've come up with the team response, go back to the client, and tell them that you've met with the team and formed with them what you can do now. It's easy to cave at this point, especially if a client is appealing to your ego. Stick to your commitments and don't overextend yourself. Show them you'll try to help by negotiating on the deliverables or timeline but protect your other account balances. The goal is to make a partial deposit. Tell them what you can do and stick to it. They may not like it, but they should respect your efforts. And if they're a favorite client, they probably have "funds" in the bank.

The next time you don't want to break the bank and you don't want to say no, pause. Ask questions, talk to your team and see what you can do, and then go back to your client and be clear about what's possible and what you can do in order to maintain all your account balances.

ALLIES

Don't forget about the key people on your support team: your supervisor, team, mentors, and optimists. They have your back, and you're grateful for the support. But do you have their backs? Is the relationship mutually beneficial? What are they getting out of it? How can you make your supervisor's day a little easier? Have you thanked a mentor lately or kept them up-to-date on your progress? Have you asked people how you can support them? It doesn't hurt to check and stay on top of it.

Develop a lifelong practice for monitoring and investing in your relationships by constantly asking yourself:

Am I making more deposits than withdrawals?

Emerging leaders who are mindful and cultivate their relationships build followers. Those who don't and only focus on results may be rewarded with money and recognition, but they're often at the top of their mountain alone. And they may not find themselves on the mountain they really wanted to reach. The leaders who have treated people well over time have a base of support who will work for them and advocate for them at critical times. Take care of your relationships, and they'll take care of you.

○ Try It

1. For the next week: Identify one bad habit that amounts to a withdrawal and don't do it. It may be barking at people when you're stressed or running late for a meeting. The key is spotting corrosive behavior and arresting yourself to get yourself into the practice of managing your behavior and making more deposits than withdrawals.

2. On a sheet of paper, write down one important person who represents your client obligations, one colleague, and one person who is an ally (mentor, supervisor, staff, optimist). Keep a journal or mental accounting of deposits and withdrawals, no matter how small. Summarize where your account balance was in the beginning and at the end of two weeks. Examples:

Dan (*assistant/support team*)

DEPOSITS	WITHDRAWALS
Asked him how his weekend was	*Yawned as he told told me*
Took time to mentor him on a project	*Didn't reschedule a check-in*
Asked for his advice on a project	*Didn't acknowledge his contribution*

Sophia (*wife/optimist*)

DEPOSITS	WITHDRAWALS
Listened to how her day went	*Snapped at her at breakfast*
Told her I love and appreciate her	*Broke a promise for date night*
Installed a light for her craft room	*Embarrassed her with our friends*

DO WHAT YOU SAY

Leadership is like third grade: it means repeating the significant things.

MAX DE PREE, FORMER CEO OF
HERMAN MILLER OFFICE FURNITURE COMPANY

When I discovered that the clay sewage pipe in my 1920 home needed to be replaced, I asked friends for recommendations for contractors. I got one bid from someone who took five days to return my call and then sent me an email with his estimate, which didn't have a lot of detail. When I called another contractor to get a competitive bid, he got back to me within an hour. Vincente with PQW Construction wanted to meet me first at the house to look at it. He showed up exactly when he said he would, took off his shoes at the door, and walked down to the basement with his clipboard. He took his time and took careful measurements and then explained to me in detail what he was going to do to disrupt as little of the landscaping as possible. I appreciated the short tutorial, not knowing what I was getting into. The next day he sent a detailed estimate, which was slightly higher than the original bidder, but I was more confident in Vincente. He called to see if I had any questions and explained his soonest availability. I signed the estimate, and when the work was scheduled, he texted the day before to make sure I remembered. He and his crew arrived on time, did exactly what they said they were going to do, finished when they said they would, and charged what he told me it would cost. There was nothing remarkable about the experience other than it had no surprises. It was remarkably unremarkable. I only wish his services included everything else I need around the house!

Say-Do Ratio

Contrast your worst customer experience with your best. People remember how you make them feel. Our best experiences stand out not by overdelivering but by simply doing what they say. There is no shortage of people who say one thing and do another. Their actions don't support their words. Over time, it adds up to not being able to count on people. Trust erodes. And without trust, why would anyone follow you? And yet, if you think about your interactions with people, how common are broken promises?

- The colleague who says they'll get back to you with some good times to meet but never does.
- The staffer who gets overwhelmed with work and lets the project deadline slide.
- The friend who promises to help you move and "spaces it out."
- The subcontractor who had to deal with an emergency and didn't get a chance to get back to you.
- The consultant who forgot to tell you what their scope covered and didn't cover.

It's remarkable how simple it is to stand out and just as remarkable that it's all too rare.

Ultimately, people want to know if they can count on you. Jay's biggest problem is his inability to meet commitments. In fact, he's reliably unreliable. You learn over time you just can't count on Jay. And while you might like him as a person and even cut him a little slack, your inability to trust him to do what he says affects how much you want to support or follow him. Simply put, your ability to consistently meet commitments is the foundation to building long-term support. Keep breaking your word and see how that works for you in the long run.

Boost Your Say-Do Ratio

Think about how well you meet commitments. Do you show up when you say you will? Do you call back when you promise? Do you deliver as stated? Here's the question to ask yourself at the end of each day:

Did I do what I said I would do?

You can build a foundation of trust by monitoring your say-do ratio, the ratio between what you say you will do and what you actually do. The more consistent you are in meeting your commitments, the more equitable your ratio will be between what you say and what you do. Promise a lot and don't follow through: poor ratio and low bank accounts. Do what you say: high ratio and healthy bank accounts.

You have an opportunity to stand out as being exceptional by critically looking at your own behavior. At the end of each day, ask yourself if you did what you said you would do. You failed if any of these are true:

- Didn't review your emails, calendar, or to-do list to see what you promised to do
- Got too busy with other things to close the loop with previous conversations
- Conveniently ignored things on your plate because you didn't want to deal with them
- Used any of the following expressions: "Sorry, I meant to." "I forget." "Time got away from me."

It's simple: Don't disappoint people. Meet your commitments. Build trust and collaboration. People will follow and support you as a leader. Here are four ways to boost your say-do ratio:

1. **Know your current commitments.**

   Be aware of what you already have out there. Get it out of your head and into your calendar or some other way of keeping track of what you said you were going to do by when. Frequently consult your calendar and to-do list throughout the day and the night before (imagine how Jay's day would have gone with a little planning). It's easy to get wrapped up in a task and simply lose track of a reminder of a commitment you made. Come up for air frequently.

2. **Don't overcommit.**

   If you call your dentist for an appointment, they tell you when they can do it. They don't bump another appointment just because you want to see them this afternoon. They have a schedule of commitments, and they honor it and expect patients to honor it too. Yet for many of us, we're much more open-ended about making our commitments. We do often bump other commitments by ignoring them or rescheduling them. Think about this: *The next time you say yes to something, to whom are you saying no?*

   Most people are so overcommitted that if a new task comes along, something else needs to move off the plate. Right before you say yes to something new, stop and pause to see if you can do it. If you can't do it, don't say yes! Say something like, *I wish I could. I want to be realistic about my commitments. I'm sorry. Let me look at my calendar before committing.* Work with folks, but don't just automatically say yes.

3. **Be realistic.**

   Be realistic about how long something actually takes. It's easy to plan out your day and be overly ambitious. Realistically, there are interruptions, things take longer than you think, life happens. Factor that in. It's better to set realistic expectations when you say yes: *I can't promise it will be done. I'll do my best. I have other commitments, and I'm not sure how long they might take to finish.* Don't we appreciate it when the mechanic is realistic about their schedule, only to finish it sooner than they said it might take?

4. Don't drop the ball.

Let's imagine you don't do what you say. You've made a withdrawal, but you've made a much bigger withdrawal if you don't communicate you haven't come through. Don't forget about people. All it takes is a quick email, text, or phone call and say, *I'm working on it. I haven't forgotten about you. I apologize.* It doesn't make it less of a withdrawal, but it doesn't make it a bigger one either.

Conserving Energy

As you move up in leadership, your commitments exponentially grow, but the number of hours in a day doesn't. You can take a different approach to working with people that preserves your emotional bank accounts, meets your commitments, and gives you a life. In the next section, I give you three new strategies to manage the constraints on your time, helping you conserve energy on your journey toward your mountain.

● Try It

1. **For the next forty-eight hours, monitor your say-do ratio.**

   - Give yourself one point for every commitment you meet.
   - Deduct one point for every commitment you push off but still complete when promised.
   - Deduct three points for every commitment you completely blow off.
   - Deduct four points if it's not the first time you've blown someone off.

2. **Look at Jay's day in terms of his say-do ratio. Yes is a deposit because he did what he said; no is a withdrawal because he didn't.**

   - His wife nudges him and reminds him it's his turn to take the kids to school, which he hasn't remembered.

     ✓ *No for not remembering.*

   - He's trying to figure out how to get them to school and not be late for a scheduled client meeting that he's already postponed twice.

     ✓ *No for postponing a commitment but partial credit for trying to avoid it a third time.*

   - He doesn't kiss his wife good-bye, silently fuming about the dog vomit and kid transport that are his commitments but have derailed his day before it's started.

     ✓ *Yes for honoring the commitment.*
     ✓ *No for being grumpy about it.*

conserve energy

73   The DIS Multi-Tool: Introduction

77   Delegate What You Can

117   Ignore The Unimportant

147   Shrink To What Works

THE DIS MULTI-TOOL
└---○ INTRODUCTION

As chief operating officer of a seventy-five-person architectural firm, Amy did everything and anything so the other principals could focus on being architects. Her door was always open, and staff came to rely on her to help them fix their problems, whether it was getting along with a co-worker, getting new software for their computer, or sharing a personal issue. Amy always made time for people.

As the office picked up bigger projects and hired more people, Amy became overwhelmed with watching the numbers and keeping her door open to any request. When the firm sold to a larger company, the demands on her time grew exponentially. New systems and processes required additional work. Her email inbox became unmanageable, stacks of papers grew higher, and sticky notes started to paper her monitor and walls. She was keenly aware that she was always behind and letting people down by not making commitments. A devoted mother, she was also determined to prioritize being there for her two active grade school-age children. The days grew longer, and her stamina waned each day.

Amy hired me to coach her and the staff on time management and communicating with teams to meet the challenges that came with rapid growth. Amy knew one of her big challenges was setting better boundaries around her time. The open-door policy wasn't working, as it took her away from other important work. For Amy, as someone who lives to serve others, saying no was gut-wrenching and felt wrong in so many ways.

Amy learned how to identify the critical tasks that needed to be done each day and protect blocks of time from staff interruptions and email requests pulling at her attention. She explained to staff that she needed focused time to work. She closed her door and closed down email for blocks at a time. She started to use her calendar more for setting aside work time rather than continuous meetings. She took herself out of noncritical meetings or made them shorter.

One Friday afternoon, when I arrived for her hour-long coaching session, she came out of her office, looking sheepish. Just twenty minutes before, she learned that the corporate office told her a major report needed to be done by the end of the day. So much for prioritizing. Amy asked if we could reschedule, and I reminded her of my "use it or lose it" agreement. I wanted to make a point:

Every time you say yes, you're saying no to someone else.

Emerging leaders like Amy continually make deposits with clients by saying yes. Their next priority is their supervisor. After those people, seemingly running neck and neck in terms of priority are their family and staff. Like so many emerging leaders I've profiled in this book, Amy was repeating a pattern by putting herself last. She said yes to everyone else and no to herself. In doing so, she was continually robbing her own emotional bank account and felt depleted. At this rate, she would never get to her mountain, which was to focus on building a great culture by developing human resource processes and hiring the best people.

The old Amy would have canceled the coaching session. After all, work always takes priority, especially over anything personal, like leadership coaching. But this time, she paused and thought about it. "Give me thirty minutes, and we can at least meet for thirty minutes," she said. She delegated much of the task to someone else, ignored the urgency of the client to get it all done today, and shrunk the deliverable to a first draft they could use right away. She told the senior manager the full report could be delivered by Tuesday, after reviewing her calendar and other commitments. She employed her DIS Multi-Tool.

In reality, it only took her fifteen minutes to write that first draft, giving her forty-five minutes to focus on our coaching session and her mountain. Today, Amy owns her own firm with two other principals and has learned the value of boundaries and not simply saying yes to everything and everyone.

Once you know your mountain and can see a clear path to what you need to do to get there, the job is to pace yourself so you stay on course and don't burn out. Amy used three strategies to do so. Together, these strategies make the DIS Multi-Tool—delegate, ignore, shrink—and now we'll examine each tool in detail. First, do some reflection to prepare.

O What Amy Learned

Use the DIS Multi-Tool:

1. **Delegate what you can.** It not only moves tasks off your plate, but it builds your team.

2. **Ignore the unimportant.** Not everything demands your full attention, either immediately or in many cases at all. Much of our days are filled with distractions and pulls for our attention that keep us from getting important things done.

3. **Shrink to what works.** You can get most things done in a shorter amount of time. Work more in triage mode, assessing what's important to do and working in smaller blocks of time to get the most important elements done.

○ Try It

1. Reflect on your day. What didn't you do that you planned to do?

2. Which undone tasks did you say no to because you said yes to something else?

3. What could you have done differently?

DELEGATE WHAT YOU CAN
⌐∘ KNOW WHAT TO SHED

When I truly was not sure what to do, I could stop, and think about whether it was taking me towards or away from the mountain.

NEIL GAIMAN

Josh loves water. Especially stormwater. As a consultant in a national civil engineering firm, when I met him, he knew something about how it flows and how to manage it for municipal projects. Well respected by his peers at the city and county, he was a busy guy. But he spent too much time in production software, computer-aided design (CAD), doing work that junior staff should be doing. Why? Because that was the way he approached projects. He knew it would get done right and on time if he was working on every detail in the methodical, step-by-step way he was accustomed to. That was the way he met his commitments and had a high say-do ratio. That was how he maintained a lot of equity with his clients. For fifteen years, it worked. But while his approach got him that far, it wouldn't get him to where he wanted to go.

Josh's mountain was to spend more time with his twelve-year-old son now before he got much older and didn't want to spend time with his dad. He could already see his son pulling away and wanting to spend more time with his friends. Josh was keenly aware of how important these father-and-son outings were to their relationship.

In three years, Josh wanted to be doing less project production work so that he could spend more time learning best practices in stormwater management. He was envious of his peers who regularly traveled around the world with a contingent of business and civic leaders to learn what other cities were doing for best practices. What were Tokyo and New Orleans doing to meet the future? He also knew that to advance, he needed to develop his network. But it was challenging to find time for lunch or happy hour with colleagues, let alone a trip. He had to turn down participating in ACEC's golf tournament because he couldn't spare the time. The managing principal fully supported Josh doing less production work and even endorsed the weeklong trips to other cities. And if Josh delegated more work to staff, they would grow as leaders, as Alison, back in "Don't Travel Alone," learned.

Nothing was stopping Josh, except how he had been working. Instinctually, he knew what he should do and what he shouldn't do. He knew the stuff he shouldn't do was weighing him down and keeping him from advancing. While his emotional bank account was high with clients, staff were being shortchanged by not being challenged by more responsibility, the firm couldn't grow without him focusing on higher-value activities, his family didn't get his attention, and he was not fully realizing his full potential as a leader and a dad.

As an assignment, I asked Josh to start each day by looking at his to-do list and current workload and asking:

What will bring you closer, not further, from your mountain?

For an example of this working to great effect, I turn to Neil Gaiman. As a young man, Gaiman didn't set out to become a rich and famous author and screenwriter. He just moved in a direction that seemed right to him at the time. Smaller, more immediate decisions. Along the way, he learned what kind of writer he wanted to be. Gaiman, who never graduated from college, offered this advice at a commencement for the University Arts Class: "When

I truly was not sure what to do, I could stop, and think about whether it was taking me toward or away from the mountain."

Josh thought about his mountain and quickly identified that whenever he was working in CAD, he was getting further from his mountain. His decision-making broke down to a simple binary choice:

- Not opening CAD? *Closer.* Opening up CAD? *Further.*
- Delegating CAD to junior staff? *Closer.* Doing it myself? *Further.*
- Coaching them to work out the solution? *Closer.* Taking back a project and doing it yourself? *Further.*

By identifying one switch in his day he could control, Josh started to see his choices more clearly. He began each day reviewing his commitments and identifying CAD-related tasks he could delegate. He met with the staff and made sure they understood the scope and expectations of delegated tasks. He stopped himself whenever his mouse hovered over the icon for the CAD software.

After six months, Josh had reduced his time in CAD from ten hours a week to one hour a week. That left him more time to spend with his son on camping trips and more time with peers on bigger, more engaging discussions about the future of stormwater management. Last time I checked with him, he was looking at joining the civic group to visit Bogota, Colombia.

O What Josh Learned

1. **Start with one routine task you should delegate.**
2. **Plan each day by identifying if you'll be doing that task.**
3. **Intentionally avoid doing that task.**
4. **Repeat until the new habit pays off and you can see forward progress.**

Check Your Pack

In the summer of 1995, twenty-six-year-old Cheryl Strayed embarked on a solo 1,100-mile trek along the Pacific Crest Trail (PCT). The PCT stretches across nine mountain ranges, from the California-Mexico border to Canada. Strayed hoped for a transformative experience that would "make me into the woman I knew I could become and turn me back into the girl I'd once been."

Strayed, an inexperienced backpacker, packed everything she thought she had to bring to have a successful adventure. Her backpack, which was nearly half her weight, was so heavy she couldn't even lift it off the floor.. "The Monster," as she nicknamed it, cut into her shoulders and restricted her from making any significant progress. Luckily, she met an experienced backpacker who went through her pack and mercilessly discarded any noncritical item to lighten her load.

Every additional ounce you carry on a backpacking journey you feel. Every additional ounce saps your energy and slows you down. A friend of mine who averages twenty miles a day on backpacking trips even drilled holes in his fork handle to save weight! Less weight equals more miles. More weight makes the journey incrementally tougher. Many tasks in our workdays are like this— items that we just carry around without really questioning if we should be carrying them. The first act of lightening your load on your leadership journey is looking at what you're carrying that it's not critical.

Taking the right steps to your mountain would be easy if you didn't have all the other stuff weighing you down and sucking the time out of your day. Unimportant stuff seems to fill every minute, leaving no room for the important tasks. The key to getting to your destination and meeting your commitments to keep your accounts full is being more discerning of what you commit to. For Josh, it was easy to find one specific task that was weighing him down. When he stopped doing that task and delegated it, he took a big step to lightening his load.

Lighten Your Load

Start by looking at each minute you spend during the day to determine if it's critical to your journey or just added weight. The only way to get to your mountain without burning yourself out is to stop doing stuff that's not the best use of your time and shift more of your time to stuff you should be doing to advance your career.

What tasks are weighing you down that you really shouldn't do?

Let's say your mountain is to "get more out of the weeds of doing the daily work." Great. What exactly does it look like to be in the "weeds"? Coordinating meetings? Answering all emails between consultants and the client on a project? Reviewing and correcting documents? Formatting documents and printing them for review? Start with a list to identify the stuff you really shouldn't be doing.

STUFF I SHOULDN'T DO
1. TAKE NOTES AT MEETINGS
2. ATTEND MONDAY CONTRACTOR MEETINGS
3. BE THE FIRST POINT OF CONTACT WITH CONSULTANTS

Lightening your workload is like cleaning the house on a routine basis. Think about when you move into a new house and enjoy that window of time when the rooms are uncluttered and the closets are tidy. Over time, you start to accumulate stuff. In six months, there are stacks of mail on the table, more books on the shelves, new clothes in the closet, and boxes of who knows what in the garage. It's a continuous process of looking at your load and eliminating things from your pack. It's not a one-time event.

Which tasks on your list can someone else do at a lower hourly rate? The law of managerial economies suggests that for businesses to run most efficiently and profitably, employees should be doing tasks commensurate with their experience and abilities. If there's someone who can do the same task that you're doing but a lower hourly cost, they should be doing it. If you're billing work at ninety dollars an hour and you shift it to someone at thirty dollars an hour, you keep overall project costs down, the client is happier, and you are free to work on higher level tasks that can also bring you closer to your mountain. Each time you refrain from doing lower-fee work, you make multiple deposits: with clients, yourself, the company's bottom line, as well as the employee who is learning to take on more responsibility. One move, four deposits.

When we have a keen sense of the right direction throughout the day—what we should do and what we shouldn't do—we can learn to make conscious choices of what we focus on, as Josh's story illustrates.

The next step in the delegation process is educating staff on why it's important they not just complete the task you're delegating but put in their best effort.

○ Try It

1. Make a list of activities that are the best use of your time and a list of things that are not the best use of your time.

2. Identify three different scenarios where you have a choice of taking you closer or further from your mountain. Examples:

   - Going to an industry networking event to make long-term business connections, critical to your success? *Closer.* Staying home to watch Game of Thrones? *Further.*
   - Fully engaging with strangers at that networking event? *Closer.* Hanging out in the shadows and avoiding people? *Further.*
   - Staying home one morning to study to receive your license? *Closer.* Allowing yourself to get distracted by email in the office? *Further.*

3. Make note of those times where you consciously make a choice that takes you closer or further from your mountain.

4. Choose one routine task to delegate.

5. Plan each day with delegating that task in mind.

6. Be aware of the trigger when you typically do the task and refrain from doing it.

7. Find a colleague and share your challenges and progress with each other.

DELEGATE WHAT YOU CAN
⌐○ OWN YOUR NEW ROLE

The role of a leader is not to come up with all the great ideas. The role of a leader is to create an environment in which great ideas can happen.

SIMON SINEK

Your biggest step forward will be when you learn how to effectively delegate tasks. Back at the beginning of the book, Nora learned when she delegated tasks that people were often better than she was at some things, and it freed up time for her to pursue marketing to elevate landscaping in the firm. Alison learned that when she let go of control, she was happier and less stressed and her team got stronger with the additional responsibilities.

When *Forbes* magazine compiled the top fifty attributes of leadership, the one skill that stands above others is influence. The most effective leaders understand and appreciate their unique role in getting more work done by engaging staff to bring their best thinking and hardest effort to projects—not by single-handedly producing work and billing more hours. Liz Wiseman, in her book *Multipliers*, said the best leaders "look beyond their own genius and focus their energy on extracting and extending the genius of others." Multipliers have a much greater impact on firms by understanding they don't need to be responsible for the final work product but instead can tap the collective wisdom and energy of the team. The less they are involved, the more that gets done and the more people grow into independent problem-solvers and leaders. The art of leadership is understanding how to affect what the organization provides to clients with minimal control of how it's done. Successful delegation is requisite to your new role.

As we talked earlier, it's hard to let go of doing something that is so personally satisfying. So much of our identity is wrapped up in what we produce each day and how we go about it. It's the gratifying part of the work: you design and build things you can see and touch. To delegate well can feel counterintuitive. Like you're losing what's given you joy and meaning. Handing it off to someone else can seem like a disservice or withdrawal to you and the client. In addition, it often mires the process to take time to teach someone else, to break it down, to coach them through the missteps to get them to a level of competency.

But each task you hold on to and don't delegate is a withdrawal with your team because you don't support your staff's growth, a withdrawal with the company for underutilizing your talents, and a withdrawal with yourself because you're not focusing on other tasks that can get you to your mountain. The need to delegate so others can grow is not unique to you or your firm. Everybody—even your client who wants only you—gets it and is probably struggling with delegating to their staff as well! Mike Baker explains it well: "Clients want us to grow in parallel with them so we can be of increasing service across a broader spectrum of increasingly complex challenges that clients face as they move up within their organizations. So, our growth is also an investment in our ability to be of increasing value to them. The stakes get higher as the challenges get more political, complex and costly. So, we need to continually develop to be ready."

In the next sections, I give you a step-by-step process that will help you assume a new role in getting work done. In the process, you'll regain a boatload of time for your list of things to do, grow your team's capabilities, and deliver work at a lower cost to clients.

⊙ Try It

1. Draw a line down the middle of a piece of paper. On the left side, write down all the reasons you don't delegate. On the right side, write down all the reasons you should delegate.

2. Share the list with a colleague who is also struggling with delegation.

3. Schedule a future date with the colleague to revisit how it's going and what you're each learning.

DELEGATE WHAT YOU CAN
⌐o CONSCIOUSLY COMMUNICATE

The problem is that once we know something, we find it hard to imagine not knowing it.

CHIP AND DAN HEATH

Successful delegation requires intentional and conscious communication between both parties throughout the project.

o **Intentional** means you're making clear communication a priority. You're not tossing a task to someone in an email. You've thought through your expectations and potential challenges. You're scheduling and not rushing through conversations as quickly as possible but taking as much time as needed to ensure effective transfer of knowledge.

o **Conscious** means you're not multitasking while you're relaying the information; you're fully aware of what you're saying, how quickly you're saying it, and when you should be talking and when you should be quiet and listening.

o **Between both parties** ensures communication isn't one-sided. You're not the only one talking. How is the person receiving it? Are they nodding and engaged or checked out and clueless? How are they approaching the project? How are they communicating progress and the ownership you want to instill in them?

o **Throughout the project** underscores the importance of continuous communication as the project proceeds, not just in the beginning. Your job isn't done once the baton is passed. Many delegations start off strong but break down by lack of regular communication throughout. You think you've been clear and don't think about it again. Or you get too busy and forget to check with the person on their progress. By the time you discover it's a hot mess, you have to jump back in and work overtime to fix it. Even when the project is done, it's productive to touch base on how it went and what you can do next time. Communication at the start, during, and after the project to debrief are critical to successful delegation.

o **Delegation** is like passing the baton in a relay race. Don't rush passing a task to someone. Make sure they clearly grasp what you want before you let go. Intentionally communicate everything they need to be successful in completing the task.

Pass Off

If delegation is like passing a baton to someone else, make sure they've got it before you let go. First, take the time to thoroughly describe what you want back in terms of deliverables. The military uses the term *commander's intent* to communicate the prime objective to the troops before a battle—capture the bridge, hold the position, etc. Things often happen in battle, but if everyone on the battlefield knows the commander's intent, or essential elements of success, they can make their own decisions that contribute to the overall operation. The commander's intent for a project might include:

o Specific deliverables and format (e.g., in triplicate, includes table of contents, has been proofread, etc.)
o Budget or allotted number of hours for their portion
o Due date for your review

Second, provide your teammate the CliffsNotes version of

what's important to the client, based on your experience. Provide past examples of work product for the client or similar clients and point out specific requirements and why it's important to follow them. A staff person needs the same information you might take for granted. Include insights into the client's personality, what they like and don't like, and past problems and successes that would be good to know.

Don't Assume Knowledge

Tom, a seasoned land surveyor, related to me the story of his first day in the field. After two hours of work, his supervisor asked him about the position of the flags on a hillside they were surveying. Tom looked blankly at the supervisor and said, "What flags?" The supervisor met his stare and immediately comprehended his oversight. "I probably should have told you about planting flags. I've done it so many times, it's just automatic." It was a lightbulb moment for both of them, one which Tom, twenty years later, still remembers when he brings new surveyors out on their first day.

How many times have you delegated a task, only to find out the person didn't have a clue how to approach it? Think back to when you were in their position and how much you didn't know—and were often afraid to admit. You were so eager to please, you chose not to admit you couldn't do it. What often gets in the way of educating others on doing tasks is skipping over the parts we assume people know. Too often, those errors of omission are not even intentional on our part.

One of the new skills you'll need to learn to get to your mountain is figuring out how to teach others. It helps to understand the four stages of learning we all go through in gaining a new skill and underscores the importance of conscious communication.

When Tom asked, "What flags?" it was clear to the supervisor that not only did Tom not know how to plant the flags but he also wasn't even aware flags were part of the job. He didn't know what he didn't know. This first lightbulb that went off was about the stage of learning called unconscious incompetence, meaning Tom wasn't even aware or conscious of his incompetence. And the supervisor also became aware of what Tom didn't know.

As soon as the supervisor asked him about the flags, the second lightbulb went off for Tom as he thought: *I didn't know about flags before, but now I do.* Conscious incompetence is that awkward aha moment when we are doing something new and having our incompetence pointed out to us. Years later, we still recount those embarrassing stories as painful lessons in our careers.

Conscious competence is about actively educating yourself about what you previously didn't even know about. You can bet that Tom asked a bunch of questions about how to properly identify and set flags after his embarrassing discovery. He might have even done research to make sure he nailed it next time. Perhaps he even created a checklist for the future that included "identify and set flags." As a new leader, you're consciously learning new skills even as you read this book!

Unconscious competence is the final stage of learning: you do the work without thinking about it. Identifying and setting flags was something Tom's supervisor just did without thinking about it. We like to think success is getting to the stage of doing something competently without giving it thought. But it's this very stage where things can go wrong in teaching others. The blind spot with being unconsciously competent is that we often forget what it's like not to know.

We can be too smart for our own good. Authors Dan Heath and Chip Heath, in their book *Made to Stick*, called it the "curse of knowledge." Great to have knowledge and be competent. A curse when it gets in the way of teaching others. After many years of repetition, Tom finally arrived at the unconscious competence stage. But when he sits down with a new employee, he intentionally revisits the first stage of learning—the lightbulb moment when he didn't know things. He remembers his own awkward experience and makes sure when he's training someone to remember to tell them about the flags.

When you ask questions and listen for the answers when delegating a task, you are being an observer of what's called the beginner's mind. You're trying to see the task from where the other person is in their competence, not where you are. You are going over familiar ground to uncover what may be hidden in plain sight because the steps and detail are no longer conscious to you. If you can successfully adopt a beginner's mind, you become a more conscious communicator, and chances are much better that delegated tasks will meet your expectations.

○ What Tom Learned

1. **Slow down the delegation process to question every step.**

2. **Check for comprehension of the steps as you go.**

3. **Think like a beginner.**

At this point, you've told the people you've delegated to what's expected and shared critical information for them to be successful. They've shared what they heard, and you've discussed any holes in their competence to do the job. There's one more step you can take in the planning stage that will help ensure success.

Double-Check

Brad Hermanson, a seasoned consulting engineer for environmental projects and a part-time instructor who teaches project management to young leaders, told me the story of how taking time up front on one project paid off throughout this career.

Brad started his consulting career in Corvallis, Oregon, at CH2M HILL. He thought he had been hired to do industrial process engineering but quickly learned he was hired to do EPA Superfund project work. One of the senior engineers in the office, John Graham, specialized in industrial wastewater work. Brad was dying to work with him and finally got his chance when John won a project with Anaheim Citrus Products. John needed some process engineering help, and Brad was available and interested.

They met, and John took the time to lay out what he wanted. But as Brad started to leave, John said, "Brad, before you begin, give me your plan." Brad was a bit surprised since nobody had asked him to do that before. He told John he understood what he needed to do, and John said, "OK, then it won't take you long to write it in a plan and give it to me. Show me what you are going to do, when you are going to do it, and how long it will take."

Brad went to his office to write his plan. He thought for a while and finally realized he really wasn't quite sure specifically what he was going to do. With his tail between his legs, Brad went back to John and confessed he couldn't quite figure out the specifics of the plan. John smiled, said OK, and then patiently worked with Brad to work out the basic ideas. They went back and forth until they had a solid plan.

Brad followed the plan and kept John appraised of his status throughout the project. The final deliverable was a home run, and Brad realized later that having John tell him to write a plan for him was the best single lesson he's had in project management.

⦿ What Brad Learned

1. Developing his plan forced Brad to think specifically about what he needed to do, and working with John on the details helped him resolve with him the best course. That lowered Brad's stress.

2. Once he was done planning, John had the comfort of knowing that Brad had a plan that he understood. That lowered John's stress.

3. John's investment up front paid off in Brad doing the job according to an approved plan. And once

John took the time to teach Brad, Brad didn't have to go through the process in as much detail the next time. He learned how to plan out a project to meet John's expectations that he could carry to future projects. Compared to a scenario in which Brad started working on John's project without some planning, the process proved to be highly cost-effective.

4. In a short lesson, John had basically mentored Brad how to plan a project and also how to effectively delegate work. He modeled for Brad how to have an intentional and conscious communication between two parties. John understood his role as a teacher and created a safe environment for Brad to make mistakes and not be afraid to admit what he didn't know.

Check for Understanding

You may think you've done a great job of describing your expectations when delegating a task. The real question is: what did the person hear? The difference between what you said and what they heard may be the difference in how well the project goes. Don't let go of the baton until you know they have it. Spend a few minutes asking some questions and listening:

- What's their understanding of what they need to do?
- How are they going to approach the task?
- What will they do first?
- What issues or challenges do they foresee?
- What questions do they have?

This is your opportunity to check to see how clear you've been as well as get a sneak preview of how successful they'll be executing the task. It's better to check if they're pointed in the right direction than to hope they are. Have them draft a plan of their approach and coach them to set up a process that will serve them well in the future.

Schedule a Check-in

Not so fast. Before you let go of the baton to let someone run with a task, set a specific time to check back in with the person on their progress. Put it on your calendar. Make it their responsibility, not yours, to follow through. Without a scheduled check-in, either it's easy to forget about checking until it's too late or you'll be anxious on how they're doing and bug them too much. Between the planning stage and your scheduled check-in is you trying as hard as possible to let them figure it out and stay out of their way. This is often the hardest part of delegation: finding that balance between helping and not helping.

⭘ Try It

1. The next time you delegate to someone unfamiliar with the client or project, thoroughly debrief and give them enough information to be successful.

2. Check for understanding before passing along a task by asking questions to see if they really grasp what you want.

3. Adopt a beginner's mind by continually looking for possible holes in their knowledge.

4. If the project is sizable, have the person draft a work plan and help them if they get stuck.

5. Schedule a check in time to check progress early in the process.

DELEGATE WHAT YOU CAN
⌐o PUSH IT BACK

**Control leads to compliance;
autonomy leads to engagement.**

DANIEL PINK

This scenario might sound familiar: After receiving a delegated task, the person emails back half-done work, saying, "Did as much as I could; kicking it back to you." You take the bait and help out and kick it back to the person. They hit another wall, and you help again. This continues until you wonder why you don't finish the project yourself.

In the classic *Harvard Business Review* article "Management Time: Who's Got the Monkey?," authors William Oncken, Jr. and Donald L. Wass make it clear: to be effective at delegating, you need to understand the hidden costs of work that's delegated. Avoid bailing people out. Keep them accountable to owning and finishing the job. If you don't want the monkey back on your back, be clear why it's important the monkey stays with them.

When I worked with her, Beth was a project manager at a small civil engineering firm. She was thirty-five, had a partner, did not have children, and liked to hike and drink local beer with friends. Her mountain was to become a principal in the firm, but that was probably seven years off. In three years, she wanted to be an associate. Beth was driven and extremely competent and loved by clients. There was nothing keeping her from getting to her mountain but herself. She fit that super-doer profile of an emerging leader doing it all herself and not asking for help. But her death grip on every detail of project management was not leaving room in her schedule for meeting with clients and prospects to develop future work. Delegation was very hard for her because she couldn't trust others would get work done to the level that people expected from her. She was stuck in her old ways, and it was keeping her from reaching her future.

Beth's goals and the company goals were the same: focus on business development to be a firm owner. But she needed to enlist the help of her support team—the direct reports she managed—to spread the load. This was tough for several reasons: First, she felt like she was burdening her team, who were already busy. It felt selfish for her to push work on to other people so that she could accomplish her goals. Second, Beth, who is reserved by nature, wasn't comfortable sitting down with her team and saying, "I want to share my personal goals and ask for your help to get there." She needed to inform her staff why they needed to do more in a way that felt natural to her style.

The next time a junior member of her team gave her a set of drawings for a new bridge, she started to take out her red pen to make corrections but then caught herself and thought: *This specific task is not taking me closer to my mountain. I really shouldn't be doing this; they should.* When she gave it back to the person to correct, she explained, "I need to spend more time on business development, so it would help if you could review these drawings more carefully."

In one sentence, Beth took several steps in the right direction: she shared the importance of getting more work for her future and the firm's; she stopped herself from doing work that wasn't going to get her there; she modeled for the junior staff person how to manage time and delegate to others; and she made the staff person more accountable and responsible for their own results, an important step in them becoming a leader. She helped her staff move to their mountain, even if they didn't know it!

How did it work? Surprisingly well. There was no pushback or rolling of the eyes. The staff person took it back and did it almost right. Beth still found two errors, but it took her less time to review it, and that small step in being clear when delegating pushed her a little closer to her mountain. Over time, what came back to her was better and better. She found more time for business development and was recently named associate principal.

○ What Beth Learned

1. Explaining why may be easier than you imagine it will be.
2. A short explanation is easy to develop.
3. Without immediate feedback, staff will not grow.
4. Find more time for your mountain by repeating this practice.

Help Make the Connection

If we look at Beth's example, we see that she took the time to explain why it was important for them to do the best job possible. In short, she was saying, "If you don't put your best effort into it, it hurts everybody." If you bring people into the delegation process with a "this is why it's important" discussion, prior to walking through a specific task to delegate, they will start to frame their task within a bigger picture to understand why they should fully own the task and do the best job possible. They'll see that their small part, such as drawing doors for a massive complex, is not insignificant. The doors are part of the overall design, which leads to the overall experience for the occupants every minute they're in the building. While they're taking care of doors, you can focus on checking with the client regularly to see if they have concerns and spend time developing the relationship for future projects. Division of labor: You have your job. They have their job. It's a team effort.

Daniel Pink, for his book Drive, studied what motivates people, particularly creative types. His research found that people are motivated less by money and more by three distinct drivers: the autonomy to be left to do the work on their own; the mastery to develop their skills and competence; and the sense of purpose that the work has meaning.

When delegating a task, take the time to cover all three motivational drivers: "I need to give you a task for you to do completely and deliver on time without micromanaging you to get it done [autonomy]. If you work on it on your own, you'll learn more and you'll be able to teach others [mastery]. If it's not done right, the whole project can be affected [purpose]. Can we spend some time going over it now, so you can ask questions, and then set a check in time for questions?"

Connect the dots to help them see what's in it for them. Remembering others' motivation is such an important part of achieving your mountain that I mention this a few times in this book. Creatives and many younger people have strong ideas of their own and want to make their mark. Acknowledge they want to be authors of their own work. Underscore that every time they prove themselves to be independent problem-solvers with the simplest of tasks, they are building confidence in you to give them a larger role. Why should you give them more responsibility to lead others if they can't master all the parts?

The work they do in mastering tasks you delegate to them is an investment in receiving more challenging, interesting tasks. On one level, people often want to be the ones with answers. They just don't always appreciate the work involved in acquiring the competence and knowledge to become the people who have the answers. How often have you heard this particularly from young staff?

- *I want the opportunity to learn more about projects.*
- *Can we have more lunch and learns?*
- *I love when we post our work and talk about it.*
- *I would really appreciate having more mentoring.*
- *Is there an opportunity for me to attend a conference on sustainability?*

There seems to be an unquenchable thirst for knowledge and sharing of knowledge. You can provide all the mentoring and training in the world, and it probably wouldn't be enough. (Recall our friend Amir, at the end of "Chart Your Course.") If people want to be more knowledgeable, frame each delegated task as an opportunity to master their skills. Say something like "If you want to help others and be a resource for interns, you need to learn how to master this task." That also gives them a sense of purpose and autonomy.

Help by Not Helping

Early in my career, I learned what Thomas Edison meant when he said genius is 1 percent inspiration and 99 percent perspiration. There's no substitute for putting in the work and figuring it out along the way.

I was hired as the country's first entrepreneurial manager of a public library, in Oregon. Huh? Exactly. No one, including me, really knew what that was about or what I was supposed to do. An advisory board of business and civic leaders came up with the idea that the library needed to generate revenue in addition to public bonds and levies. Put in a coffee shop. Start a volunteer run gift store. And dream up some other stuff. Develop a plan and make it happen. That was as much guidance as I got.

On my first day, I sat in my small, windowless office (the administration building was the former county morgue) and looked at the thick concrete walls. And my computer. And back to the walls. I had to figure out my job without help. I didn't have John, from a few pages ago, to help me work through my thoughts. My job was to invent things to do, without a template. I can still relive that discomfort in an instant. What if an idea implodes and I'm seen as a disappointment? How do I measure success? What do I do first?

I clawed my way through figuring it out: jotting down thoughts, organizing ideas, creating a spreadsheet with a matrix to weigh costs and benefits, meeting with people with answers, touring other libraries, reading online (pre-Google in 1996), presenting ideas to the library director, adjusting to realities, and working with vendors, consultants, and attorneys to make all the ideas reality.

Five years later, the California Library System hired me to teach other libraries what I did in Oregon. The University of Washington paid me as an adjunct professor to teach librarians the concepts of entrepreneurship and marketing.

The best education you can get is through trial and error. Venturing to be wrong. Learning as you go along. The ground between knowing and not knowing, between conscious incompetence and conscious competence is fertile. When you delegate a task to someone, remember when you've learned the most. Was it when someone gave you the answer, or was it from the perspiration of struggling to find the answer? For employees to have greater mastery and more autonomy from you, they need time to use their own brain. You may be inclined to want to bail them out as soon as they have an issue, but you may be robbing them of a learning opportunity.

Once you've given them the task, keep the monkey from jumping on your back again. If they come back with questions or say they've hit a dead end, encourage them to figure it out, rather than jumping back in and rescuing them. Keep it in their court as much as possible and remind them that autonomy and mastery are best learned without you spoon-feeding them every detail of each step along the way. They need the opportunity to figure it out on their own.

Explain Why

The leader's responsibility is articulating the why to the team— both for your development and for theirs. That's a foreign skill for project managers who are more accustomed to producing outcomes than influencing outcomes. It may feel awkward to have a "why conversation" with staff, but I promise it won't kill you.

Use your own words in explaining why they need to own a project and follow through. Avoid the conversation at your own peril. Don't be surprised what happens if you don't do anything. People won't naturally make the connection. They may be inclined to give a half-assed effort. They may think it's below them and not get around to it.

Be clear and help them see why every task is important to their development and the organization.

○ Try It

1. Revisit your mountain and identify the key tasks that will bring you closer and what tasks you shouldn't do.

2. Identify specifically what people need to do to complete tasks and why it's important for them, the firm, and your mountain.

3. Compose a simple sentence that captures what you need them do and why it's important. Brevity is the key. Avoid making it personal, blaming, or emotional. Keep it about the task at hand.

4. Appeal to the desire to work autonomously and be the authors of their own work.

5. Explain how mastering this task is important to you trusting them with greater responsibility.

6. Show them how this task is linked to their overall success and an integral part of the project.

DELEGATE WHAT YOU CAN
⌐₀ ASK GREAT QUESTIONS

Is this your best work?

HENRY KISSINGER

It's natural and even commendable that people new to tasks want to avoid making mistakes. They don't want to bug you (small withdrawal), but they really don't want to screw up and let you down (big withdrawal), so of course they want guidelines on what's OK to do and what constitutes an understandable mistake versus a big, uh-oh kind of mistake.

For your part, you want to encourage them to figure it out, but you also can't afford for them to burn time on a project going down the wrong road. There are two critical steps to give them clarity, foster autonomy, and keep the project on track: tell them how much decision-making they have and schedule a check-in to review progress and guide them toward successful completion.

Authority Audit

The high-tech industry factors small failures into the research and design process so engineers have license to learn what works and what doesn't. The only way to innovate is through trial and error. If you're not failing, you're not pushing the boundaries. Small failures are opportunities for people to learn along the way to figuring something out so they can come up with something that's innovative. But it helps if people know how much room they have to make a mistake. What are the limits of their decision-making? What are they responsible for, and what are you, as their manager, responsible for?

A colleague of mine, Gerry Langeler, who has run several successful high-tech companies and operated a venture capital firm, developed a way to answer those questions, for every instance. He learned early in his career the importance of establishing an "authority audit" between a new manager and supervisor. It helps a staff person figure out how much autonomy they have for any one delegated task, from high authority or power to lowest authority or power:

1. *I decide on what to do, act, and do not need to inform my manager.*
2. *I decide on what to do, act, and then let my manager know what I did.*
3. *I decide on what to do and go to my manager, and we discuss and arrive at a collaborative decision, and then I act.*
4. *I recommend what to do to my manager, my manager decides what to do, and then I act on their decision, if asked.*
5. *I alert my manager to the issue but take no position. It is my manager's call to make.*

"The goal is to identify the kinds of decisions that will come up so that the staff person understands not only their responsibility domain but their authority domain and limits," says Langeler. The authority audit also creates a clear progression for someone who wants to advance. If you're starting out at a Level 5, you understand that you need to start asserting your recommendations for approval to get to Level 4. And your supervisor also knows it's their responsibility to provide those opportunities for you to stretch in your competencies.

As an emerging leader, you can use an authority audit to help make clear the level of responsibility you are granting your staff.

Providing more clarity can help tame the delegated task monkey by reducing the need for constant check-ins and questions.

Scheduled Check-in

Reviewing progress and not taking it back may be the hardest thing you'll do while delegating work. Remember that your job is not to do the work but to influence the outcome. That requires patience and willpower not to reassume complete responsibility. Think of this as an opportunity to build your emotional intelligence by exercising greater self-awareness of why it's hard to let go and managing your emotions and behavior about not finishing something to your exact standards.

When Liz Wiseman studied the most effective leaders, she learned they don't really manage people as much as guide them to find the best solutions and do the best work. It's tempting to come in with "here, let me just tell you how to do it." But you'll never grow their competencies or your own career if you're doing the work. Check your inclinations. Try a soft, general question like:

How's it going?

There are a million ways to answer that. You're letting them decide how they want to present their work so far. You're encouraging them to be authors of their work. High school math requires students not just to come up with the right answer but to "show your work." Your job is to listen, observe, and ask questions as your team member shows their work.

The check-in will be much more powerful for both of you if you replace a response with a question. Instead of "That's not right," ask, "Why did you take this approach?" Let curiosity be your guide. You're the learner, trying to figure out their decision-making process. Other great questions:

- *What have you tried?*
- *What haven't you tried?*

- *How does that solve the issues?*
- *How could you raise the level of work?*
- *What are you going to do next?*
- *What resources do you need?*
- *Where are you encountering difficulties?*
- *What are the biggest remaining issues?*
- *What are your next steps?*

Asking great strategic questions turns out to be the key feature of the best leaders: the ones who transform organizations, as Brené Brown explains. When we take the time to fully explore project problems and ask questions, we uncover new ways of looking at problems and new solutions that not only solve the issue but also "break apart conceptually complex ideas and reveal our capacity for greater strategic thinking."

Best Work

Former Secretary of State Henry Kissinger could be demanding. Winston Lord, ambassador to China in the 1980s, once drafted a speech for Kissinger. When Lord handed it to him, Kissinger asked, "Is this your best you can do?" Lord took the draft back and worked on it some more. He brought it back to Kissinger, who asked again if that was the best he could do. This back-and-forth continued, until finally, on the ninth draft, when asked if that was the best he could do, Lord said yes, that was the best he could do. Kissinger replied, "In that case, I'll read it now."

Is this your best work?

All too often, we accept work that needs work. Maybe the person knows you'll want to add your touch to it. Or maybe they didn't try hard enough. In posing the challenge to Lord, Kissinger taught him a valuable lesson: push back work that could be better. A senior civil engineer asks his staff, "Would you put your stamp on this work?" People are motivated to perform at their best when they feel pride in their work and feel that it is respected and has meaning. Don't deprive them of the opportunity. If you accept work that is not at the highest potential, you are supporting a "good enough" attitude. If you ask them if it is their best work, you are encouraging them to put in their best effort. Push for excellence.

○ Try It

1. Have an authority audit conversation before you start.

2. Ask questions and listen.

3. Challenge them to do their best work.

4. Keep it in their court.

DELEGATE WHAT YOU CAN
⌐⟶◦ ACCEPT THE ACCEPTABLE

I'm not here to be right. I am here to
get it right.

BRENÉ BROWN

When I first met Terry, he was one in a team of eight emerging leaders in my leadership class. I was struck by his eagerness to learn. Here was someone who realized that he didn't have all the answers about leading people. Not knowing and being vulnerable enough to admit it turned out to be one of his greatest strengths.

Terry was one of the smartest and most competent architects I'd met. He was great at designing and executing every detail of a project. Clients loved him. He relied on two skills from his toolbox: work hard and control everything. He was convinced there was just one way of doing things: his way. After all, it had worked well up to this point in his career. But that was when he had his own boutique firm, could do whatever he wanted, and directed people to follow his orders. Not exactly an empowering place for new leaders who had ideas of their own.

When he moved to a larger firm, his job changed from doing to leading. He was told in his first review that while he was technically strong and great with clients, this job required him to grow his team. He needed to guide and coach them—a very different muscle for Terry. He had to let go of being the author of his own work but support and guide what others produced.

After two years of hard work and following the delegation process I outlined, he was named principal. He said, "Once I realized my identity wasn't 100 percent defined by my technical skills, I found great satisfaction in helping my team grow. When I realized how powerful that was, it was the best feeling. Like giving gifts is better than receiving. Like feeding the hungry. Seeing what we can do together." His big reward at the top was seeing how far his influence had changed not only his team but himself.

After a year and a half of coaching, Terry was promoted to principal in the firm. He did it by not having all the answers but by being open to other ways of getting to the solution. The old Terry thought: *I'm right. You're wrong. You're too stupid to understand my point.* He learned that being the smartest person in the room doesn't always win friends and foster collaboration.

He summarized it like this: "Just because I think I'm right doesn't mean I am. There's no right answer in architecture. Instead, it's shades of gray. How do we build consensus? That's the challenge of being a leader. Not right or wrong. Yes or no. . . I can pose this to twenty different architects and get twenty different answers. How do we build consensus? How do we take the pieces as a group and take it to the next level and make it better? What if, what if. Changing your thought because you're open-minded. That's where the magic happens. It's a we, not a me. And I think that's a big part of really being a leader."

○ What Terry Learned

1. There's more than one answer.
2. You can have a bigger impact by not having the answers.
3. Leadership is often questioning yourself.
4. There is power in serving others.

Letting Go

You won't be effective at delegation and making it to your mountain, if you maintain a death grip on the final outcome. Imagine what it must be like for someone to take a project you've delegated to them and do it exactly the way you would do it. That might seem like the best outcome. But is it really? Who says your way is the right way? The client? Your years of experience?

If your staff has complied with the commander's intent and the client is happy, accept the acceptable. I sometimes get a lot of push back on this point: "So, you're advocating to stamp work that's sub-par, that's not right, when the client is paying us for my expertise?" Of course not, but much of what's acceptable is subjective. It's in your mind and makes sense to you, but it may not be as important to everyone else. There may be more than one acceptable solution.

You may believe your value is 100 percent tied to getting it right. After all, there's strong evidence that producing predictable results and making clients happy has brought in money and got you recognized as a model leader for others to follow. Ask yourself this when reviewing someone's final work product:

Am I uncomfortable with it because it's not the way I would do it?

Our egos often kick in, as Terry's story illustrated. I experienced this recently while coaching a team of four people to teach my communication class. I gave them the script and coached them to follow it. Initially, they followed it to a tee. Then they started to improvise and veer off course. It wasn't what I had in mind, based on what I knew from many years of teaching the material. But I caught myself and thought: what is the overall goal here? If it's to make them into in-house trainers, comfortable and confident in teaching the concepts, then they were meeting the commander's intent. I backed off and let them go.

In the AEC industry, getting it right and doing it my way can mean even more. Often the work that's done has big implications: the wrong design can implode a multimillion-dollar project or compromise the integrity and safety of the structure. This is not a leadership class, after all; this is a twenty-story building or a bridge. The risks are real.

The art of learning to be a leader in this industry is knowing what's critical to get right and what's acceptable to do differently. I'm not an engineer and architect, so I'm always careful to add a disclaimer to my advice: use your best judgment in what's right and what's acceptable. My coaching clients who struggle with this have found it helpful to start backing off gradually. If it's acceptable, let it go. Find someone in your firm who has mastered the balance of *get it right* and *get it done* to help you let go of perfectionism. Don't be too hard on yourself. The temptation to put your mark on work is like that rubber band that will snap you back to the wall, keeping you from moving forward. Just be aware of what it's costing you each time you do it.

The Trap of the Knower

In your new role of motivating others to take ownership of their work, it's important and scary to step away from being the one with all the answers, as author Brené Brown says. It's tempting to think: *I am the only one with the answers. I am the only one who can do this right. After all, if I'm not in there knowing, what's my value?* Terry wrestled with these questions. Not knowing is often the opportunities for transformation in both ourselves and others.

We like to think that success is arriving at the ultimate stage of learning: unconscious competence. We just do things beautifully without thinking. But as we've discovered the curse of knowledge can get in the way of seeing what we're missing when teaching or communicating to others. The curse of knowledge can also get in the way of new thinking that only comes from collective decision-making. Collaboration and teamwork are at the heart of any strong organization.

Delegate What You Can

1. Know What to Shed
2. Own Your New Role
3. Consciously Communicate
4. Push It Back
5. Ask Great Questions
6. Accept the Acceptable

If we adopt more of a conscious competence model of always working on knowing—not having the answers but searching for better ones—we also leave room for solutions by other people that just might be better than the ones we've done many times before.

Successful delegation centers on intentional and conscious communication throughout the project. If people understand the limits of their decision-making and honor the check in session, you'll both grow as leaders. If you're clear on why it's important for them to take ownership, you also need to be honest with yourself that you need to let go of ownership.

Your real growth as a leader is not knowing the answer but fostering new ways of getting to solutions by supporting others.

○ Try It

1. Learn to let go of control and accept work that meets the commander's intent.

2. Debrief with the person after the delegation to see how it went and seek honest feedback on how to improve next time.

3. Seek a colleague or mentor to help you work through what to delegate and how to let go of perfectionism.

4. At your next team meeting, have an open conversation about challenges and solutions for better delegation. You don't need to have all the answers. Just ask good questions.

IGNORE THE UNIMPORTANT
⌐..o KNOW WHAT'S IMPORTANT

If the mind falls asleep, awaken it. Then if it starts wandering, make it quiet.

RAMANA MAHARSHI

Josh, the stormwater engineer, realized his traditional approach to work as a doer was limiting his evolution as a leader. To adopt a new way of working, he had to stop himself and think about his next move. Opening CAD took him further away from his mountain. Delegating CAD to a junior person brought him closer to his mountain.

What Josh had to do was ignore his impulse to open CAD, the way he had hundreds of times before. He had to ignore what was comfortable and familiar to focus on a new way of doing the project, which was uncomfortable and unfamiliar but ultimately the right move for his mountain and everyone else.

For a while, choosing to ignore his old approach was deliberate and mechanical. But over time, that thought process of stopping and delegating CAD became ingrained. A new habit had formed that served him better in the long run. The process began each time he was faced with a choice to open or to not open CAD. If successful delegation hinges on intentional and conscious communication, the very act of delegating starts in the mind as an intentional and conscious decision to ignore a task and instead delegate it.

The Mystical Post-it

Kent was a principal architect, with thirty years at the same firm. He'd lived through a lot there, including a lot of changes. Quiet and reserved, he was known for his technical expertise. He enjoyed the role of fixing complex project problems, but he had little patience for people's problems. He also didn't relish the politics that so often accompany managing an office. Still, he couldn't ignore the feeling that his experience and analytical skills could make a big difference in helping to lead the office. He could play a much more significant role as a mentor to people if he could devote his time to higher-level problems and not just addressing specific technical questions.

When a firm leadership opportunity opened, Kent had a choice. He could stay at a lower, more comfortable level and avoid the hassles, or he could push himself to step up into a less comfortable role as a leader and make a bigger difference in the future of the firm. He decided now was his time to make the switch and reach higher.

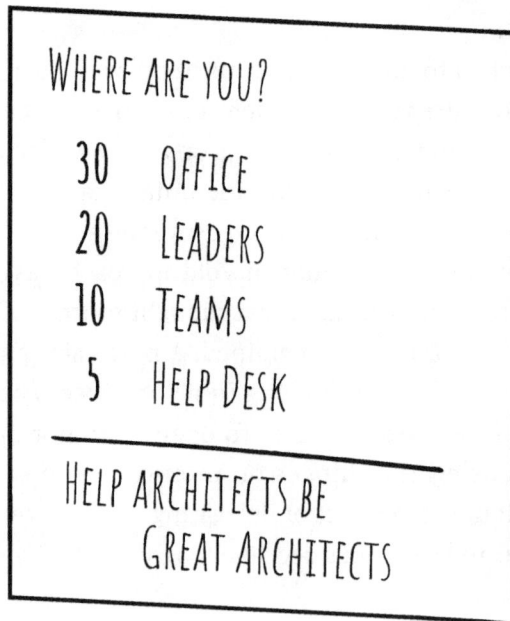

WHERE ARE YOU?

30 OFFICE

20 LEADERS

10 TEAMS

5 HELP DESK

HELP ARCHITECTS BE
GREAT ARCHITECTS

He needed to remind himself, like Josh did, what would bring him closer or take him further from his mountain. He wrote up a Post-it note and put it on his monitor to keep himself focused.

In order to get to the top of his mountain, "Help Architects Be Great Architects," Kent broke down how he was currently spending his time and how he needed to spend his time.

- **5,000-foot (5) Help Desk:** At this level, Kent was providing technical support for individuals on specific project issues. As the most technically knowledgeable person in the firm, it was important for him to be available to more junior staff, but it was not the best use of his talents.
- **10,000-foot (10) Teams:** The next level up would be making sure team leaders had what they needed to run their projects and discussing specific issues to keep people engaged and productive. Here, Kent would have more impact and greater influence but still be mired in projects.
- **20,000-foot (20) Leaders:** If Kent really wanted to make a greater difference, he should spend more time strategizing and coordinating with the other two office leaders on office-wide staffing recruiting, budgeting, and planning that would help improve communication, culture, and profitability. The office had been operating in market-sector silos rather than as an organizational whole. Management was flat and decentralized, which meant no one was tracking staff utilization and profitability. In short, management wasn't entirely sure what people were currently working on, much less what they should be working on. This level of activity would elevate Kent's impact and influence.
- **30,000-foot (30) Office:** The highest level for Kent to have the greatest impact and influence would be leading systemic changes that would improve not only today's profitability but also tomorrow's. Designing flow charts and spreadsheets to capture a better process for tracking

schedules and utilization and profitability would really elevate the office and help make great architects. This would mean researching best practices and talking with people who were the most knowledgeable.

If he wanted to increase his influence, his focus and time needed to be less on projects and more on processes and people. The simple sticky note gave him a simple matrix to help remind him each day what tasks had the greatest impact. Helping others was better than working alone. Helping teams rather than individuals was reaching even higher. Coordinating with the office leaders had an even greater impact than working with teams. And focusing on big organizational initiatives would transform the office the most and elevate everyone. The best use of Kent's time was at the 30,000-foot level.

It would be nice if he could afford to ignore everything else, but he couldn't. He needed to continue to bill enough time directly to projects. People still needed help, and he needed to spend time with other leaders so they were coordinating efforts and acting as a leadership team. It was all important, and that was the issue that many emerging leaders found themselves in. Everything seemed equally important. It was challenging to find time to focus on higher level activities.

Kent learned it can be easier to focus on important higher-level tasks and ignore less important tasks if he simply paid attention to what he was doing at any moment. At the top of Kent's note, he asked himself:

Where are you?

That was Kent's alarm clock to wake himself up from time to time. Kent's day was full of choices of how he spent his time, but he became more mindful of what to focus on and what to ignore by simply being more conscious of what he was doing and then being more intentional about his next move.

The simple system worked for Kent. He "magically" began to find more time for higher-level work because he became more conscious of how he was spending his time and then choosing to sometimes spend it differently. He planned each day by setting small goals for 30,000-foot work and working less at below 5,000 feet. He ignored his impulse to take on the help desk role. He didn't immediately jump to answer someone and, instead, let them figure it out.

Three months after starting, he told me it was going OK. After a thoughtful pause, he said, "I haven't opened up a project in three weeks!" Instead, he had spent that time developing a master schedule for staffing time on projects for the next six months. His impact and influence increased the more time he spent at higher levels. By keeping people busy and making money for the firm, Kent was indeed seeing that he was "helping architects be great architects." A year into his Post-it experiment, the office became the most profitable among all fifty-four offices in the company. Kent had scaled his own mountain with a note.

O What Kent Learned

1. Identifying and grouping tasks is a helpful way to start.

2. A visual reminder is a simple and powerful trigger to wake yourself up.

3. Pausing to think during the day can help you make better decisions.

4. Mindfulness is enough to make the switch.

Wake Up

The wealthiest people in the world are keenly aware that time is limited and time is money. You better believe that Warren Buffet and Bill Gates know and value every minute they spend and consciously make choices of how to spend it and not waste it.

Start by being mindful of what you are doing and ask yourself, as Kent did, "Where are you?" Over time, you'll become increasingly mindful of every minute that passes and make wiser choices of how to spend it.

When I ask workshop students what they've put into practice since the last class, they typically report they can't point to a specific win, but they definitely thought more about what we talked about in the last session. They may report that while they spent too much time on production work, they were more aware they made that choice. They slipped into saying yes to every request, but each time they said yes registered with them a little more. They started to pay attention to how much they said yes. Something was imprinted on their minds that wasn't there before: awareness of an unconscious, autonomous response that wasn't helping them advance.

Leadership is about being more conscious about your interactions and how you use your time. What you do and what you don't do. It's about making choices. And as Kent's and Josh's stories illustrate, stopping to think before acting is the first move. Mindfulness is the practice of staying awake. It's being aware of where you are at any one point in the day so that you're not asleep but awake.

On any given day, how would you answer Kent's question: "Where are you?" Are you conscious of what you're doing in the moment or about to do, or is it a blur, a mad rush? If you're not aware, you're asleep at the wheel. And if you're not conscious, you're not making informed decisions that will build equity in your relationships and maximize the time in your day. What's true for you?

As an emerging leader, you'll often find yourself between two of the four stages of learning: between unconscious incompetence (not knowing what you don't know) and conscious competence (actively working on improving your skills). So, turn up your awareness of what you don't know.

Practice being more aware by bucketing typical tasks. Those in the low-level bucket are project work, or doing. Those tasks in the high-level bucket are organizational focus, or leading. While you

Conscious/Awake

Can account for how you spent your day.
Keenly aware of the clock.
Know when to wrap up a conversation.
Know precisely when you make a withdrawal.
Make a deposit in real time.

Unconscious/Asleep

Don't know where the day went.
Lose track of time.
Get lost in a conversation.
Find out later you made a withdrawal.
Miss the opportunity to make a deposit.

need to balance both, knowing what you're doing during the day and how it relates to your goals is critical to evolving as a leader. Here are two more examples:

Linda
- 5,000-foot level: designing projects
- 10,000-foot level: guiding a project designer
- 20,000-foot level: organizing group critiques/shares
- 30,000-foot level: establishing design standards and process throughout the office

Bill
- 5,000-foot level: project management
- 10,000-foot level: red-lining and quality control

- 20,000-foot level: team mentoring and education
- 30,000-foot level: business development and marketing

What are your levels?

In the next chapter, I walk you through how to sift through the demands on your time by determining what's immediate or urgent versus what's important.

O Try It

1. Identify your buckets of tasks by 5,000-, 10,000-, 20,000-, and 30,000-foot levels. The higher the level, the closer it is to the best use of your time.

2. Write on a sticky note one sentence that captures your mountain's summit.

3. Write "Where Are You?" on the note and put it somewhere you'll see it most of each day.

4. Talk to a colleague about how it's going and what you're observing.

IGNORE THE UNIMPORTANT
⌐o KNOW WHAT TO IGNORE

What is important is seldom urgent and what is urgent is seldom important.

DWIGHT D. EISENHOWER

Rebecca's career as an architect had been guided by meeting the expectations of others. She was good at following the path prescribed by others and keeping full the bank accounts of clients, management, and staff. She did what management told her she could and couldn't do. Even though she wanted to be a project manager, she was told she had to first become a project architect. Rebecca would have to put in the time, get the experience, learn the skills, just like others had. She believed she was capable of the next level, but she lacked confidence to advocate for herself.

One day, things suddenly changed when senior leadership left the firm. Within the vacuum, Rebecca was now considered a candidate to step immediately into senior leadership. Did she want to be a principal to help lead the firm? Was she ready and capable, given that all this time she had been told she belonged a few rungs down on the promotional ladder? Questions and doubt almost consumed her.

Rebecca jumped into the challenge, with the encouragement of the new managing principal, who told her he believed she was ready and capable. Confidence didn't come easy or quick. Rebecca continued to question whether she deserved the position. She continued to look for external validation and followed what others expected. But mentorship and answers were not always readily available. She would have to figure things out as she settled into the role.

Rebecca questioned what was important to her and what kind of leader she wanted to be. "I had to learn not to fit into someone else's shoes but be authentic to what felt right," she told me. For instance, in management meetings, colleagues would put Rebecca on the spot and want an answer to a question right away. "I need time to think about things. I had to learn to be more assertive and tell them I knew what they wanted but they'd just have to wait." Rebecca decided it would be a bigger withdrawal to acquiesce to their sense of urgency if she wasn't confident with her response. It was more important to make a withdrawal by not responding right away than by compromising accuracy. She was willing to defend her process—an important step in finding her own center and gaining confidence as a leader on her own terms.

As a mother of two young children, Rebecca didn't want to sacrifice family time for work, even though it was necessary at times. She continually monitored if a withdrawal at work was truly worth a withdrawal at home. When she was a project architect, her workload was more manageable. There were fewer competing demands on her time, but in her new role, it became more important to draw boundaries and say no more often. While saying no before was an easier decision, saying no now required more consideration of the consequences. The decisions were more nuanced. Saying no to working late also meant walking by the desks of her peers who continually worked late. They never said no, but she was done defining her path by what others did and said. Saying no meant disappointing colleagues, who had come to rely on her habitually saying yes. But saying no to her family felt equally bad. Occasionally working late was fine, but long bouts of dragging herself home, missing dinnertime, and being unable to stay awake when her kids read at night was unsustainable. Rebecca learned to make finer distinctions with her time. "I would say to myself, this looks a lot like other situations where I said yes to work and regretted it later. I'm not doing it again. I'm going to ignore my impulse to say yes."

Rebecca found that saying no to colleagues was easier when she had an honest conversation with them about her boundaries. "I don't want to say yes and not bring 100 percent to the project." They may not initially have liked her saying no, but they grew to appreciate that she had boundaries and clearly communicated when and why she said no. Because she was maintaining her say-do ratio, which I discussed in "Do What You Say," she increased their trust in her even as she said no to them.

> ## ⊙ What Rebecca Learned
>
> 1. **Ignoring people isn't always a bad thing.**
> 2. **Leadership is a constant tradeoff between deposits and withdrawals.**
> 3. **Urgent isn't always important.**

Urgent and Important

Promising leaders get ahead because of their competency and attitude. Their say-do ratio is high. They are reliable and responsive, often responding to everything right away, making deposits all day.

But as Rebecca's story illustrates, that kind of pace is simply not sustainable. And it keeps you from focusing on important tasks that could both help you and your company in a larger way. You need a way to prioritize so you can distinguish between tasks that require your immediate attention and those tasks that can wait.

Urgent tasks demand our immediate attention. Important tasks have greater significance. We live in a world where we often get the two things mixed up. We want to know something, so we Google it and get the information immediately. We want to know if our partner can pick up eggs from the store, so we quickly text. We even get frustrated if the internet speed is slow and the page takes a few seconds to load or someone doesn't text us back right away. In many ways, we are addicted to a sense of urgency, driven by the speed of technology. We want it now, no matter how unimportant that thing is. Our clients are not immune to the sense of urgency. They are constantly trying to get things done sooner. They want answers now. We don't respond to their email right away, so they text us.

As the World War II Allied Forces Supreme Commander and, later, the president of the United States, Dwight D. Eisenhower knew about urgency and importance. He said, "What is important is seldom urgent and what is urgent is seldom important." Urgent doesn't always equate with importance.

Decades later, Stephen Covey developed and popularized this idea by illustrating it in four quadrants in *The 7 Habits of Highly Effective People.*

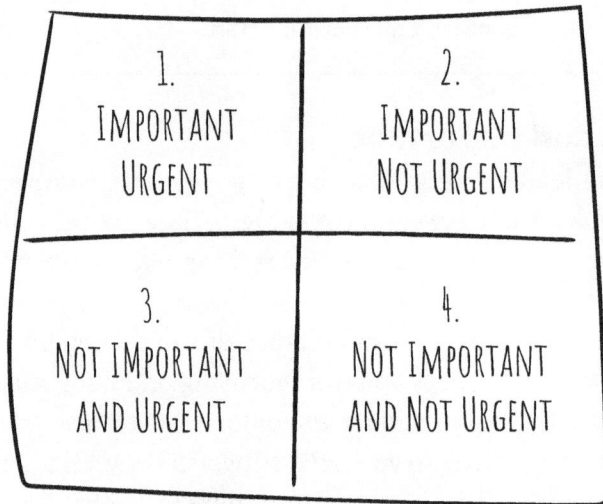

1. IMPORTANT URGENT	2. IMPORTANT NOT URGENT
3. NOT IMPORTANT AND URGENT	4. NOT IMPORTANT AND NOT URGENT

QUADRANT 1: IMPORTANT AND URGENT

These are time-sensitive tasks that if ignored have real consequences: The 5:00 p.m. deadline to submit a proposal for a forty million dollars project. The client meeting at which you'll be presenting your design concept. Your child's last soccer game. The award dinner for your partner. Make these a priority. Important and urgent tasks often impact our social bank accounts the greatest, particularly as withdrawals when we fail to prioritize them.

QUADRANT 2: IMPORTANT AND NOT URGENT

Pull out your list of things to do to get to your mountain. These are definitely important tasks: identify jobs we should delegate, take time to mentor a younger staff person on a technical task, write a sympathy card for a friend whose father recently passed away, and schedule dance lessons with our partner to reconnect. But because they are not urgent, we tend to ignore them. They also are often self-generated ideas rather than represented by someone in front of us demanding our attention, so these tasks easily dissipate into thin air. We would be wise not to ignore them. Important and not urgent tasks often impact our accounts greatest as lost opportunities to make deposits. Importantly, these tasks are ones that make the difference between an OK life and a great life. Make these a priority and schedule them to make them urgent. Quadrant 1 and Quadrant 2 should be your priority for the simple reason they are important. Everything else is just noise to be ignored and managed so you can stay focused.

The most successful business leaders regularly schedule important-but-not-urgent time. George Shultz, who at one time held the positions of Secretary of State, Secretary of the Treasury, Director of Management and Budget, and Secretary of Labor, in addition to serving as an executive at engineering giant Bechtel Group, understood the value of time. He also understood he had to deliberately set aside time to get out from under the grind of work in order to expand his vision from what was right before him to what might be possible. Shultz regularly chose an hour in his day when the only people who could disturb him was his wife and the president. He found a quiet space and closed the door. The only thing he had was a notepad, pen, and his imagination.

QUADRANT 3: NOT IMPORTANT AND URGENT

When you start to quantify where you spend your time during the day, you'll be amazed at how much of it is in Quadrant 3: tasks that are not important but are urgent. Recall the key questions we asked earlier to steer our decisions throughout the day:

Is this the best use of my time?
Is this taking me closer to my mountain?
What should I not do and delegate?
Where am I?

All of those prompts are designed to help you avoid the trap of responding to the Quadrant 3 distractions: emails, texts, and similar interruptions. No wonder people working from home during the pandemic are more productive. There's less noise to pull them away.

Quadrant 3 is all that stuff that comes at us that we respond to because (a) we've trained ourselves to auto-respond to any text or email; (b) we think it's more efficient to respond right away rather than let it pile up; and (c) we want to be responsive and make a deposit. Try asking this question next time you receive a text or email or someone wants something from you:

Do I need to respond right away?

Quadrant 3 tasks are only urgent because they are in front of us, and many times, the urgency is driven by someone else's emergency. While they may be important to respond to eventually, they don't typically warrant breaking from our schedule of important work to respond to right away.

This is a prime opportunity to use the ignore strategy of the DIS Multi-Tool. Your first impulse may be to think it's a withdrawal to ignore someone's request. It's not that you are totally ignoring them, but you are taking more control over what constitutes as important enough for you to respond. "Anything less than a conscious commitment to the important is an unconscious commitment to the unimportant," wrote Covey.

Let's say that you've chosen this moment to turn off email and your phone and have found a quiet place to reflect like George Shultz did by closing his door (good for you, by the way!). What exactly happens when people can't get an immediate response from you? Any number of things: they figure it out on their own; someone else answers it; the request changes with new information; or new tasks become more urgent for them.

Even if someone texts you—multiple times—or stops by your desk, your schedule doesn't need to constantly bend to the demands of others, unless it's Quadrant I. If it feels disrespectful to ignore them, just tell them you're in the middle of something important and you'll get back to them. Write it down, so you don't forget, or ask them to schedule an appointment, so you get an invite.

Before you decide to respond, ask yourself if this is a task you should really delegate. If it's not critical that you do the task, delegate it and save your energy for important tasks. Once you do delegate, recall that your job is to ignore all those "what about this/what about that" requests from people you want to coach to be more self-reliant. It is important to define work you can delegate each day, to take the time to debrief with the person, and to make time for the scheduled check-ins. But it's not important—in fact, it's counterproductive—to get pulled into helping them out whenever they ask for it. Quadrant 3 is often the slippery area where what we think is a deposit costs in multiple ways as withdrawals.

Our default is to interpret no as a withdrawal. Saying no to your supervisor sounds ill-advised. But what if your supervisor invited you to be on a subcommittee for a topic you've expressed interest in? When you look at your promised commitments, you realize you can't take it on without dropping commitments and making withdrawals. Besides, there are already a lot of people on the committee. And you assume your supervisor asked you because she wants to support your interest and wants to make sure you're not left out. But this qualifies as an invitation, not a necessity. Instead of just accepting the email invitation, you drop by her desk and say, "I'd love to join that committee, but I don't want to drop the ball on the Kohl's expansion, and I've got other commitments I can't ignore. I'm going to pass, if that's OK with you." You didn't ignore the email, but you chose to be more direct and explain why you were saying no. Your supervisor has a better understanding of your choices and should respect your decisions. Be more discerning about what you say yes to or focus on. Ask yourself:

Is this truly a withdrawal if you ignore it or say no?

People often include us in emails or ask us to attend meetings without really weighing if our involvement is important. There's a tendency to just include people in email and text threads and meetings, either as a courtesy or out of habit. It's not necessarily a withdrawal to ignore things where your involvement isn't clear and your absence won't be missed.

QUADRANT 4: NOT IMPORTANT AND NOT URGENT

This is easy: stop doing tasks that are neither important nor urgent. Think about all the time consumed by mindless things like getting lost in Facebook, watching stupid animal videos, and reformatting documents with a new font even though no one is going to see them. And while it's important to bond with coworkers on a personal basis, be aware of how much time consumes discussions that are not important and not urgent. Don't get me wrong—we all need to check out with some mindless activity from time to time, but watch the clock. Quadrant 4 represents wasted opportunities to focus on meaningful Quadrant 2 tasks. In this quadrant, we make the greatest number of withdrawals with ourselves and others by squandering the opportunity to make steps toward our mountain and putting deposits in our accounts.

The idea here is to focus most of your day on things that are important rather than just urgent. The next time you see an email or text or someone coming over to take over your schedule, ask yourself:

Do I really need to do this right now?
Is this the best use of my time?
Is this taking me closer to my mountain?

If the answer is no, get back to your important work.

Be Mindful of the Important

The big insight that Rebecca had was she had to determine what was really important and then manage around her commitments so the withdrawals she did make didn't erode trust and confidence in the people she interacted with. Think back to Amy, from the beginning of "Conserve Energy": You have more options than yes or no, as Amy figured out. Her first impulse was to cancel her coaching session with me. After all, she didn't think it was wise to say no to her manager. But she found a way to compromise and make a partial deposit by delivering the most important part of the report right away and ignoring the impulse to do it all.

Dig a little deeper into what's needed to see if you can make a partial contribution to a project without sacrificing other priorities. Ask what's important to deliver right now and why. Be creative and collaborative about how you can contribute on a smaller scale—thirty minutes of your time rather than three hours. Balancing your accounts is a constant process of evaluating when to say yes and when to say no and how to maintain relationships.

Let's look at some common scenarios to see which quadrant you would put them in and why.

o **Taking the time to plan your week?**
First, is it important? Certainly, but is someone else driving the action, or do you need to schedule it and take

the time? It's Quadrant 2 because it's important but not urgent. Make it urgent by scheduling it so it gets done.

o **How about if you receive a text from someone wondering if you received the email you just read?**
Is that important enough for you to respond to? It's urgent because someone is texting you, but it's not important to respond to. Chalk one up for Quadrant 3.

o **Do you respond to a routine email reminder about the weekly staff meeting?**
Is it important? Is it urgent? No, Quadrant 4, not important and not urgent, but how often do we respond with something like, "OK, got it. I'll be there." It might seem like a little thing, but these little actions add up and can drain our day if we're not conscious.

o **Taking the time to call a client to tell them you're running late to a meeting?**
Important? Yes. Urgent? Yes. Quadrant 1. If you don't do it and forget, there will be consequences, so do it.

---

o **Try It**

1. The next time you receive an email, text, or any other demand on your time, ask yourself: do I need to do this right *now*?

2. Become more aware of Quadrant 4—not important and not urgent tasks. Eliminate time wasters.

3. Schedule important tasks each day to move yourself further in your career and life.

IGNORE THE UNIMPORTANT
⌐⋯o IGNORE DISTRACTIONS

Your focus determines your reality.

GEORGE LUCAS

One day, I arrived for a coaching session with a project manager. The receptionist said the project manager was wrapping up a call and would be out soon. From my seat, I could see across the office to where my client was immersed in her call. As she hung up, she glanced at her computer screen and dove into, I assume, responding to an email. And then someone came up to her desk to ask her a question while she was typing. After fifteen minutes of observing her, I decided to approach and remind her of our appointment. She literally jumped out of her chair. "Oh, my god, I forgot about you. I mean, I didn't. I had our meeting in my calendar until a client called, and then I tried to answer somebody's question. I got distracted!"

Sound familiar? Microsoft conducted a study and found that every interruption costs us about fifteen minutes of productivity— whether we are being interrupted or we are breaking from a task. Part of that loss is due to the time it takes to recover and refocus on the task. But they also found that it's often a new distraction, in the form of a new email, text, call, or someone wanting our attention, that pulls us away.

Because time is finite, we often try to cram as much in as possible. We believe we can handle it by multitasking: thinking and doing many things at once.

What we commonly refer to as multitasking is better described as task-switching. The brain is not capable of intently focusing on two serious tasks at the same time, explains productivity psychologist Dr. Melissa Gratias. "Our brain does not perform tasks simultaneously. It performs them in sequence, one after another," Dr. Gratias says. "So, when we are multitasking, we are switching back and forth between the things we are doing." When we split our time and jump back and forth, we risk losing details and the power of our focus. We lose the thread of thinking that makes great design possible. At the end of the day, we end up with a pile of unfinished work that we need to revisit the next day and remember where we left off.

Time Blocking

Working in blocks allows your mind to stay focused on similar activities so you can make the connections, follow the threads, catch the details, and find what some call the flow of work. When we choose to work in blocks of time, we gather up tasks that are connected so our attention and mindset are concentrated in one mode.

Kaylee, a project assistant at a civil engineering firm, felt bad bugging her manager each time she had a question. She began a practice of writing down her questions on a legal pad and then scheduling a convenient time with the manager to review all her questions in one block of time. There were several benefits to this approach: some questions became resolved as she did the work on her own; it gave her more time to think about the questions and come up with her own solutions; she found other ways and people who could provide answers; and when she did meet with her manager, it was more efficient because he was focused on addressing her questions rather than distracted and not present. Kaylee was being more intentional and conscious about her communication. She also made a positive impression on her supervisor, which only built more support for her as an emerging leader.

Email Tyranny

It would have been easy and tempting for Kaylee to send an email to her supervisor each time a question occurred to her. Email has become part of our thought process. Get an idea, send an email. The problem is that sending, reading, and responding back to email creates a vicious loop. Inboxes get clogged, people get overwhelmed, things get dropped, messages get misinterpreted. Email is a great tool, but if it's not managed efficiently, it can dominate our day and rob precious time from getting work done.

A study at the University of British Columbia tested the validity of time blocking for email by comparing two test groups. Participants in group A checked their email three times a day and then closed it down to focus on other work. Group B participants could check it whenever they wanted. What they found is that group A spent 20 percent less time working in email than group B. When we simply respond to emails as they arrive in our inbox, we don't discriminate between those that require immediate attention and those that simply show up. When you wait to check email less often, you reduce the back-and-forth of emails. The time you spend not engaging and being distracted is time you claim for more important things.

Four Types

There are four types of time that can help you be more productive, meet commitments, and conserve energy:

1. **Focus**

   During this type of time, you need to be fully engaged and focused on content and details. You're engaged in the things that make you money or get essential tasks done—like applying your critical skills to a problem for a client, facilitating a staff meeting, or editing a proposal. Instead of answering every email as it comes in, you might organize all the emails for a specific project and comb through all of them at once to understand a progression of changes in a specific phase; assemble all your time for your timesheets at once; develop the team's schedule for the week by focusing on people's calendars and factoring in vacations and other conflicts. In your personal life, it's helping your son with his homework or talking about daycare plans with your partner without checking your text threads for project updates. Reserve focus time for your highest use.

2. Buffer

This is all that time that impinges on focus time, which we often don't account for: preparing for a meeting, traveling, checking email, and fielding questions from staff. When our calendars are packed end to end with focus time, like meetings, there's no buffer time for the things that naturally happen. Factor in buffer time to maintain quality focus time.

3. Reflection

This is time to step back and see where you're going and how you're doing, as you did when creating your mountain. You're reviewing your vision, planning the next quarter's goals, envisioning steps for the next week, and reflecting on how you're spending your time. Howard Schultz, CEO of Starbucks, and Oprah Winfrey follow the practice to reflect daily on what's going right and what they want to achieve. To get to your mountain, you need to regularly check your course to stay on the path.

4. Free

This is down time to recharge. Free time is just that. Time for you not to do work and to give yourself a mental break and tune in to what you need: a walk, a nap, lunch, playing cards with your partner, catching up with an old friend on the phone, playing soccer with your kid in the backyard. Even Elon Musk of Tesla takes time to recharge from his busy day! Use free time to bring balance into your life to keep your energy level up.

Recap, Redirect, Reschedule

When we're interrupted by colleagues, our instinct is not to ignore them. Let's say somebody comes up to your desk and they just want a quick second. You're deep in a proposal; you can't be interrupted. You know it's going to take more than a quick second. But how do you say no nicely to staff interruptions without upsetting people?

Before you give away your time, do this: stop and quickly assess the situation.

Is this a good time?
How much time can I spare?

If you don't have time, explain why. Most people will take a cue and come back at another time. But if somebody insists that it'll just take a second. . . well, you know, nothing takes a second. So, set some limits. Tell them upfront that you have five minutes, so when that "quick second" stretches much beyond a minute or two, you can politely wrap it up. A good way to do this so the other person knows they've been heard is to recap the conversation. Then tell them you need to get back to work and physically shift or move away from them. If the issue really is going to take more discussion, you can reschedule it for another time. Make sure that they see you putting it in your calendar. You can also redirect them to somebody else. Most people want an easy answer. They'll accept what you offer in the moment along with rescheduling or redirecting, and really, they usually figure things out on their own anyway.

It's not always a withdrawal to ignore what's urgent.

Setting a vision and getting there is all about managing the moments of your day. Be mindful of how you're spending each minute and make intentional decisions to focus on those things that are important for you, the people you care about, and your company; ignore everything else in your way.

○ Try It

1. Schedule blocks of time and manage distractions so that you're focused on one thing at a time.

2. Turn off email and only go into periodically.

3. If interrupted, recap the conversation to end the conversation, redirect or reschedule conversations if you're focused.

IGNORE THE UNIMPORTANT
⌐⋯o DON'T IGNORE PLANNING

**Your mind is for having ideas
not for holding them.**

DAVID ALLEN

Mark manages construction crews that repave asphalt on highways in Oregon. Because half of the year is rainy in Oregon and asphalt and water don't mix well, the dry summer months are when most of the paving is done, primarily at night when traffic is lighter. It's dangerous work with big equipment, hot materials, traffic screaming by you, and lots that can go wrong. Much of Mark's day feels like everything is equally urgent with little time to even eat or sleep.

Mark is one of those reliable, agreeable construction managers who never says no and who races to get back to people when they call, text, or email. And it was killing him. Literally. The stress of always being on and feeling like he needed to answer people right away was taking a toll on his health. What had gotten him here now wasn't going to get him anywhere further than a heart attack.

Most of the demands on his time came from five key team members who reported to him. While he couldn't control all the IM, texts, calls, emails, and live, impromptu meetings that came at him during the day, it was easier and had a greater impact to start making changes with people who reported to him. He tried a different approach to his day that gave him more control and, ultimately, more peace of mind.

Mark called a meeting with his five people and defined what constitutes "it can't wait" and "it can wait" requests for his time. They agreed that most things could wait for at least a couple of hours. Mark said they would have a check-in each morning and a couple scheduled check-ins during the day. That allowed almost everything to be addressed at a planned meeting rather than as an interruption.

Mark started his day by planning the schedule. He then convened his team for the morning huddle. These ready-set-go meetings were purposefully short, only about twenty minutes, but they helped set the priorities for the day with the team. There was only one question that each person addressed: what was their plan for the day?

Mark made sure these morning huddles stayed on point and didn't become problem-solving discussions that would drag the meeting out or whining sessions where people complained about unreasonable schedules or problem clients. What was their plan for the day? That was it.

This accomplished several goals: it kept people accountable to their stated priorities; it kept Mark in the loop in terms of what his team was working on and their progress toward completion of projects; it helped Mark set boundaries of his time; and it did it efficiently without a bunch of vague, confusing emails being tossed back and forth. "We all know what we need to do. Let's do it and talk again later in the day." People refrained from bugging Mark until 10:30 a.m., the next scheduled check-in, and then again at 3:00 p.m.

That was all Mark needed for some breathing room to make his schedule for the day, have lunch uninterrupted, and get some sleep. When people refrained from being spontaneous, they started to work differently and solve problems on their own. When they did check in with Mark during those scheduled times, they were more organized and efficient in their communication.

This strategy required Mark to ignore the team members who hadn't fully embraced the new time management system. It still left people outside his team—clients, vendors, and subcontractors—wanting an immediate response, but over time, Mark learned how to ignore urgent messages and field only the truly "it can't wait" requests.

○ What Mark Learned

1. Not everything is equally urgent. Most things can wait.

2. Scheduling time reinforces people working in blocks.

3. Ignoring is not a withdrawal if you have made an agreement before.

4. Clear team communication is essential to greater productivity.

Plan Your Day

Kris leads a successful mechanical contracting firm. His days are jammed with making sure projects are running smoothly, estimating new projects, answering technical questions, meeting with his controller over budgets, managing a transition to a new software system, and talking with HR about revamping their employee orientation process. Ambitious and high-energy, Kris is also renovating his vacation home and planning a two-week excursion with his wife to hike the Alps. Kris used to start his day by picking up his phone from his bed stand and answering emails and then responding to everything that came at him in the moment. The pace of his day never stopped until it was time to go to bed. He was exhausted and worn out. Many of the higher-level tasks that he should focus on were lost in the mad rush of the day. One day as he was looking over mechanical drawings for a hospital, he had an insight from engineering that could help him with how he approached his days.

Mechanical contractors install the heating and air-conditioning systems in buildings. These are not your home-size units but equipment the size of a pickup truck that sits on top of commercial buildings. When electric motors first start up, the starting torque is much higher than when it's fully running. A soft start is a device used to temporarily reduce that load to extend the life of the motor. What if Kris could install a soft start to his mornings so they were more gradual and didn't give him whiplash with the sudden force of the demands on his time? Maybe it would help reduce friction and stress if he started more gradually and ramped up.

Kris's version of a soft start begins in the morning with coffee and quiet reflection on his back porch as the sun comes up. He thinks about his day and his biggest priorities. He reviews his commitments in his calendar and looks at his to-do list from yesterday. He takes out a pad of paper and creates the day's to-do list of what he plans to do and when. He puts a star by the two 30,000-foot-level tasks that are essential to complete. He also makes sure to include getting back with people, even if he needs to move deliverable deadlines around. Kris understands that his greatest impact and influence is focusing on people over projects. If he supports them, they'll do the work.

Soft Start

The biggest challenge that emerging leaders face is structuring their time so they get important things done each day. Spending just twenty minutes in the beginning of the day creating a game plan makes all the difference between chaos and getting the right things done. How do you start your day? Do you feel like you are shot out of a cannon and rush into the day in a mad frenzy? Or do you have a thoughtful, working plan that reflects what's important to your relationships and your growth as a leader? Ignore anything else until you have a plan for the day.

Whatever system you want to use—a pad of paper or a fancy app—get your to-do list out of your head. Carrying that stress of remembering it all reduces your ability to think creatively and your capacity to be mindful of how you're spending your time.

Ignore the Unimportant

1. Know What's Important
2. Know What to Ignore
3. Ignore Distractions
4. Don't Ignore Planning

Save some brain cells for important work and get your reminders out of your head. If you start your day without a basic battle plan, it's easier for your day to be hijacked by emails, texts, and interruptions by people wanting your time. Sure, stuff happens, and plans change. But you'll get more accomplished if you at least are working from a game plan and schedule.

Once you have a plan for your day, hold a very short, standing meeting with your team (no more than fifteen minutes) to huddle on the day's priorities. This gives you a quick accounting of where people are and what they said they were going to do. It also helps the team coordinate on projects so everyone knows what the other person is doing. If a person tries to hijack the meeting and problem-solve an issue, ignore indulging them. Don't let them derail the focus of the morning huddle.

⦿ Try It

1. Start your day with a soft start to review your commitments and determine your priorities for the day. Be mindful of not taking on too much but being realistic about how much time you have in the day.

2. Identify what you can delegate.

3. Block off when you will do your tasks.

4. Write it down so you can review it throughout the day.

5. Meet with your team for a morning huddle to compare priorities for the day. This is a quick, focused, ready-set-go meeting. People can call in if they can't be there in person. Have as many of these in a week that make sense to you and your team to stay focused and productive.

6. Work in blocks throughout the day to increase your productivity and conserve mental energy. You want to conserve your best thinking for those activities with the greatest impact and influence.

7. For the next couple of days, try closing down email, reopening it periodically throughout the day, and then closing it down again.

SHRINK TO WHAT WORKS
⌐···o TAKE SMALL STEPS

The journey of a thousand miles begins with one step.

LAO TZU

Even if you master delegation, ignore distractions, and focus on the important, there still isn't enough time in the day for all the ingredients for a balanced, successful life. There's always another meeting to attend, email to answer, or task to complete.

Time and energy are finite. But how much of our days are well spent? The 80/20 rule tells us 80 percent of the value of most things comes from 20 percent of the effort. Delegation helps you get things off your plate. The ignore strategy helps you focus on the important. The shrink strategy means we can get a lot done in a short amount of time, if it's spent well. Shrink goals down to the ones that are doable; claim every little win you can claim; work in small, focused blocks of time; do the best effort in what time you have available, not what others dictate; and learn to let go to get things done, without chaining yourself to doing things perfectly.

Lily is a project engineer for a midsize commercial contracting company who wants to advance to become a senior project manager. Her mountain is to work as a project manager on a large school project in the next three years. She attended one of my leadership workshops, wrote out her mountain, and enlisted the support of a team of people, including her supervisor. Lily identified that she needed to expand her network with colleagues, particularly young women like herself. She realized that to grow in her position, she needed to learn about business development and decided to dedicate some time to it.

Business development was daunting to her. She wasn't a big drinker and had no interest in golf. Both of those activities seemed to be where most networking got done. She'd rather walk her dog in Forest Park and hang out with friends in her backyard. Lily started her day with a soft start, like Kris in the previous chapter. Every day, she wrote down, "business development," on a Post-it and even wrote some action items:

- Join Rotary.
- Find a mentor who can help me connect with more people.
- Consider hosting a small gathering to watch a local baseball game.
- Take a colleague out to lunch.

But Lily wasn't making progress in getting anything done for business development. Even with time blocking, her regular project management duties took away any time she had identified for business development. A colleague who took one of my time management classes suggested she make her goals smaller and more specific.

Instead of all those goals, which were too vague and too long to achieve, she identified just one small thing for the week: contact Claudio, a project manager at ZMA Architects, for lunch. To make sure she did it, she put a deadline of "by Wednesday" and put it in her calendar as a to-do item.

The lunch with Claudio turned out great and much more comfortable and productive than meeting at a bar at the end of the day. He had some great insights into the client they were working with, including an imminent leadership succession. Since the daughter of the owner was going to be taking over in the next couple of years, it would be important to develop a better relationship with her. Claudio also told Lily about a new AIA committee for emerging leaders that was hosting networking events with colleagues.

○ What Lily Learned

1. One small goal is better than a big list that doesn't get done.

2. Shrink goals to their smallest elements, e.g., "have lunch" becomes an even smaller goal of "set it up."

3. Lock each goal into your calendar, to make it a to-do item.

4. Just as lunch with Claudio was not just good for Lily's company but for Lily's mountain, your goals may also do double duty.

Make Small Goals

Mountains can be like resolutions: Exciting to make. Not so much fun to actually accomplish. *I'm going to go home by 5:30 each day. I'm going to do that fishing trip with my son. I'm going to be a senior associate and have a greater say.* We get a lot of satisfaction just from making a goal. It feels like we've made a huge step in the right direction by the very act of making up our mind and hearing ourselves say it. The euphoria hasn't cost us anything. We didn't have to make some sacrifices to get it. Like getting up to go to yoga instead of sleeping in. Like studying to get our license, instead of watching Netflix. Like anything that sounds like work!

To design goals that are small enough to get done, follow a system first outlined by George Doran, Arthur Miller, and James Cunningham in a 1981 article "There's a S.M.A.R.T. way to Write Management Goals and Objectives." SMART steps are: Specific. Measurable. Achievable. Relevant. Time-bound.

SMART

SPECIFIC
MEASURABLE
ACHIEVABLE
RELEVANT
TIME-BOUND

Here are some actual SMART goals developed by some students in my workshops:

- Take an hour and read capital improvement plans for Lake Oswego and report future opportunities to the team by next Wednesday.
- Schedule monthly lunch meeting with Beth to support each other by end of the week.
- Read for twenty minutes about integrated design delivery Tuesday morning at 7:30.
- Spend fifteen minutes researching associations I might join by January 31.
- Walk a total of five miles by Sunday.

SPECIFIC
Identify steps that are specific, ones you can see and hear. Imagine if someone has a video camera and is recording your actions of your mountain-making activities. They should always include an action verb so the camera can see it. Reread those examples:

read, report, schedule, walk. Compare that with using verbs like *think, consider, be aware.* What does it look like to think? Instead, use verbs that are observable. When you add detail like "capital improvement plans for Lake Oswego," you're being more specific than "research business development opportunities." It has teeth because you've identified exactly how you'll be spending your time. You won't be wasting it trying to figure out what to do. You've got a specific task you can write down and check off when done.

MEASURABLE

You should be able to measure or quantify your goals. Peter Drucker was right when he wrote, "What gets *measured* gets *managed.*" Put your steps into numbers like above: one hour, fifteen minutes, five miles. If you train for a marathon, you set measurable goals: weight train on Monday for thirty minutes; increase from five miles to six miles. It's no different in setting SMART goals. You could have said that you would read about integrated design, but making it twenty minutes helps you in estimating how long you can take on a task and helps make it more concrete in your mind.

ACHIEVABLE

With all the demands on your time, the only way to carve out for tasks that you feel take you away from other obligations is to make them small enough to achieve them. My rule is the smaller the block of time, the better. Note the action item: "Schedule monthly lunch meetings with Beth to support each other by the end of the week." That probably takes less than a minute to do and is something you can fit into your week. You could have easily said, "Schedule five lunch meetings with peers for support." That might have felt good to make a big resolution, but you don't have time for all those meetings. Choose one thing you can do. Think fifteen minutes here and there. Still too much time? Try ten, five, even one minute is better than nothing!

RELEVANT

This is the only test: will this step take me closer or further from my mountain? When you look at your to-do list for the week, how many of your tasks are relevant to where you want to go? If you have your mountain clearly defined in front of you, it helps you see if tasks can get you there. The new leader who identified "take an hour and read capital improvement plans for Lake Oswego and report future opportunities to the team by next Wednesday" had been told in his recent review that if he wanted to become department head, he needed to bring in more of his own clients. Becoming department head was part of his mountain and taking an hour to do specific research was definitely relevant to getting to his mountain.

TIME-BOUND

The best way to ensure you'll do a task is to give yourself a timeline when it will get done: by next Wednesday, by Friday. Ideally, get as specific as possible. Remember the example: "Read for twenty minutes about integrated design delivery Tuesday morning at 7:30."

○ Try It

1. Write out two SMART steps for the next week. Keep them small enough so they can be done in fifteen minutes or less. Make them particularly specific and relevant to your mountain as opposed to something you need to do.

2. For the next week, try a soft start by reviewing your commitments and planning your day, prioritizing one SMART task that will get you closer to your mountain.

SHRINK TO WHAT WORKS
└─○ COUNT SMALL WINS

**If you don't like something, change it.
If you can't change it, change your attitude
about it.**

MAYA ANGELOU

In a traditionally male world, young Philomena, aka Phil, a
project manager for a construction firm, had a steep climb to
scale her mountain of becoming a stockholder and owner in the
company. She had two qualities, however, that gave her decisive
advantage: she was disciplined and perennially upbeat about any
situation.

Phil's current position doesn't come with a lot of authority.
Much of the day she feels like it's best to do what she's told. She's
come to accept that there's a lot outside of her control. But that
doesn't stop her from showing initiative and her ambition to learn
and develop herself. She's no fool. She can see and sense that the
guys don't easily let her into their social circles. She chose this
field and knew it would be challenging, but it's also rewarding
to build things. Even when she was a girl, she was using power
tools and helping her father with household projects. Rather than
get angry about it, she takes what she can in terms of wins and
marches forward, claiming any credit for what she can do.

Still, Phil is wise enough to understand that life is not just
about working hard. She needs a life too. Every Monday at 7:30
a.m., she has a recurring planning appointment with herself. She
sits down and opens a Google document called Weekly Planning

to look at what she said she was going to do. Phil then opens a document, Weekly Progress, and records any success or win that's helped her get closer to her mountain.

- Volunteered to present project at the firm's next lunch and learn.
- Invited myself to sit in as two senior project managers discussed a budget issue on a project.
- Resolved a major scheduling conflict with two subs and got the project back on track, garnering praise from Tim, the owner.
- Delegated administrative work to an intern.
- Met with a friend for a run in Forest Park and drinks afterward.

Phil could easily focus on what isn't going well and how little she's accomplished toward her intended goals. But what would that get her, other than depressed? Taking care of yourself means consistently and constantly filling your own emotional bank account. Beating yourself up: withdrawal. Building yourself up: deposit. The reason Phil is successful is that she understands the power of having a full personal bank account. Her ritual of writing down what's going well is her way of staying strong and positive. It's not a natural mindset. It's a mindset she consciously and intentionally builds and maintains.

O What Phil Learned

1. **Creating a practice of recording small wins creates a positive mindset.**

2. **No one will do it for you because no one else can see what's relevant for you.**

3. **Small wins add up and reinforce the desire to get more small wins.**

Count the Progress

I start my coaching sessions with emerging leaders by asking them what progress they've made. The question often lands on them like a bomb. Instantly deflated, they slump in their chairs and look like they've let me down because they didn't do what they said they were going to do. It's like they're reminded of all their personal failures: lack of discipline, inability to say no, slipping into old, and unproductive habits. When we shoot high, we can get in our heads and beat ourselves up that we've failed by falling short of our goals.

The mind can be a dangerous neighborhood to be left alone in.

I know my job is not to beat them up any further but build them up. I ask them questions and probe for any change in approach or any small step in the right direction. I'm looking for progress and positive focus. When I hear it, I repeat it back to them and give them a "good job!" I want them to feel better than when we started.

Author Dan Sullivan writes we can easily change our attitude about our progress by recalibrating what we measure. The left side of the diagram represents how we typically set goals and measure progress: We start by visualizing the ideal outcome or your mountain. We set goals toward the mountain, but we then routinely focus on how far we still have to travel to get there. Measuring the distance between here and there can seem daunting and discouraging. The gap can suck us in like a bottomless crevasse. It doesn't help us continue to set SMART goals and move forward.

Sullivan suggests instead that, as we continue to hold in our mind's eye our ideal outcome, we focus daily on our gain between where we started way back in the beginning and now. As a coach, I'm looking for the gain as a motivator. For example, I might say to my client, "The old you would have said yes and regretted it.

The Gap

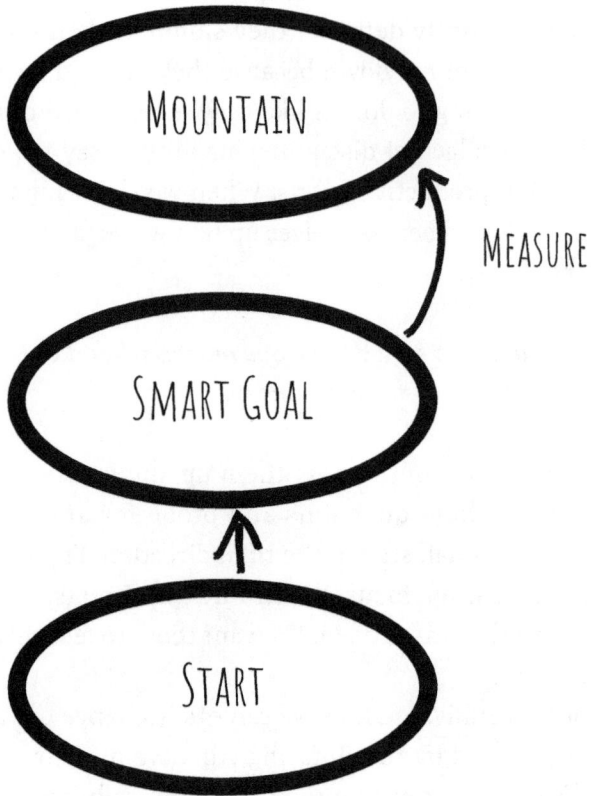

Saying no yesterday is success." And: "Even delegating some work last month is a step in the right direction." Or, "Even though you wanted to do a morning huddle with your team every day, it's progress that you're meeting twice a week. That's better than not doing it!" Small wins add up.

Phil discovered a long time ago that her success depends on what she does, not what comes to her. If she wants to be positive, she needs to practice positive conversations with herself. She doesn't look at the gap of what she did not do in a week but takes credit for the gain of what she did do. If her goal was to read once a week for an hour, but she read for only twenty minutes, that's

THE GAIN

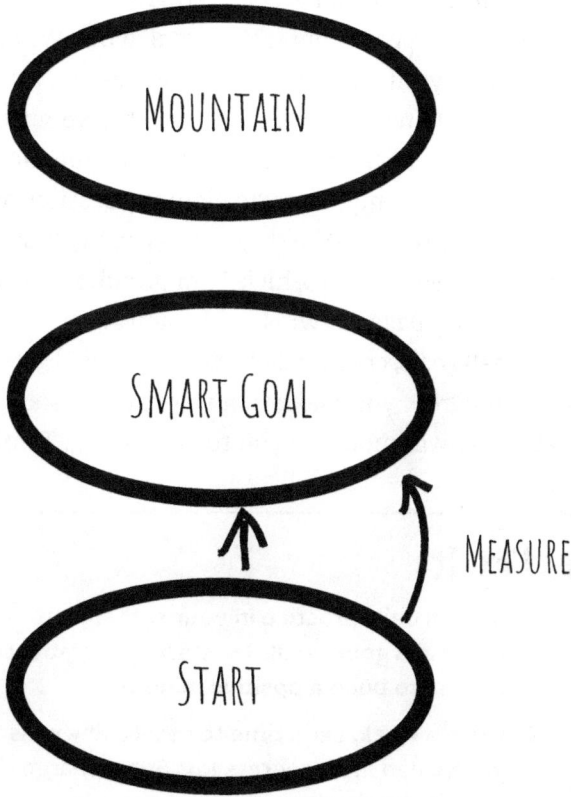

still twenty minutes more than she did before setting the goal! She might have easily fallen into the gap of feeling like she hadn't gotten as far as she wanted. But because she developed a practice of setting small goals and recording her progress each week, she gave herself full credit for the work she had done. When you can't recall wins, you can't take credit. You've cheated yourself out of a hard-earned accomplishment.

I started doing this practice of recording my small gains after attending a leadership program developed by Sullivan. One rainy day while sitting in a coffee shop, I was having one of those lousy weight-of-the-world days that comes with being a solo entrepreneur. I was feeling defeated, having fallen into my own gap of how far away I was in reaching my mountain. I opened my Google document entitled Weekly Progress and discovered I had recorded eighteen pages of weekly small wins! Wow, I did all that?! I surprised myself and immediately felt better. No doubt, if I hadn't recorded them each week, I wouldn't have remembered or been able to draw from those successes as a morale booster. Each quarter, when I do my strategic planning sessions with two other consultants, I review Weekly Progress as my first step and identify the top three wins of which I am proudest. (By the way, it's now up to eighty pages of wins, and counting!)

If you set small goals, create a daily game plan, and give yourself credit for any progress you make in a week, you'll soon create a positive habit that will motivate you to keep going. Think small.

⦿ Try It

1. Make a daily practice in your soft start to reflect on what's going well. Try starting a gratitude journal to build a positive mind set.

2. Once a week, set a time to record any wins you've had in a progress log. Supercharge the process by sharing your progress with a peer. Look back over your total wins from time to time to give yourself perspective of your total gains.

3. Be aware of how much you give and don't forget to do things for yourself, even if it's for a few minutes to take care of yourself. Enlist the help of people, like Alison did (in "Get Support").

4. Write down the things you can control and what you need to learn to accept. What actions can you take that might influence how others perceive you?

SHRINK TO WHAT WORKS
⌐○ SHRINK TO FIT

I've written several books in 15 minute increments.

DIANA ABU-JABER

There are times when delegating and ignoring don't suffice. You need to give certain tasks your attention. Even if they're not that important to you, they are to other people—particularly those you report to. After all, to keep your bank accounts full, you can't let people down and make constant withdrawals. You need to maintain your say-do ratio so people know they can count on you. How do you fit in everything while still coming home for dinner and having a personal life?

The answer is to shrink your effort to do the best job you can within the available time you have. We often accept and work within time blocks other people assign to us. But how much do you really get done in a day? Remember that the 80/20 rule suggests that, many times, 20 percent of effort results in 80 percent of what's important.

Triage

Rich Mitchell, who led Mackenzie, an architectural and engineering firm in the Pacific Northwest, preached a simple mantra to young project managers who struggled with not having enough time:

How can you do the best job within the amount of time you have?

He learned the value of working within a budget in his teens at a local supermarket chain. Rich worked the 4:00 a.m. to 1:00 p.m. shift, restocking the shelves to make it look fresh and appealing to shoppers the next day, bringing items out from the back of the store and labeling them, putting them on the shelves. It was a big store with a small crew and limited time to do all the work.

On typical shopping days, it wasn't a problem to accomplish the job. But on heavy days like Memorial Day weekend, they simply couldn't fully stock all the shelves. That often meant only restocking shelves as best they could—three cans of tomato sauce deep, for instance, rather than the ideal eight cans deep. And when time was tight or inventory was low or when someone unexpectedly called in sick, Rich would do his best and walk briskly down the aisles and look for holes in the shelves and at least bring inventory up to the front so there was at least one deep, giving the shop that well-stocked appearance. A practice that was dubbed sh#tfacing. Not ideal, but you do the best job you can within the amount of time you have. You optimize for maximum impact.

⭕ What Rich Learned

1. **Not all time is equal.**
2. **Prioritizing higher-value tasks boosts your productivity.**
3. **Quick tasks often provide the greatest benefit.**
4. **Shrinking requires being intentional and disciplined.**

Now, when Rich comes home from vacation, he takes stock of the neglected yard work. Rather than rolling up his sleeves and doing it all right then, he asks himself: *how much time do I have, and what's the best use of that time?* If he has an hour, he'll mow the lawn. If he has two hours, he'll also edge, pull some weeds in the bed, and use the leaf blower. If he has three hours, he'll tack on pruning the shrubs. He works in a triage mode, evaluating what he can do within the time he has that will return the greatest benefit (optimizing for maximum impact given the time constraints). Mowing the lawn is the highest, and pruning is the lowest.

Mark, the paving manager in "Ignore," used a shrink strategy with his team by keeping the morning huddles to a maximum of twenty minutes, limiting check-in times to twice a day, and maximizing check-in times to three minutes. As a result, people used their time well, were prepared, and got to the point. He also used triage with his phone by only checking it occasionally for any fires that needed his attention. Mark was able to regain about three hours a day by using the ignore and shrink strategies.

We have seen how shrinking time in email and working on focus time helps us stay present and productive. When I give people a ten-minute break during a workshop, most people immediately take out their phones for email or messages—even before they might need to go to the bathroom. I've only given them ten minutes, so they are forced to work in triage mode, scan quickly for important messages, and respond to the ones that need a response. Time's up. Phones off. If I gave them twenty minutes, they would still be on their phones that whole time, and claim to have needed it, but when given less time, they managed to work in triage mode, using the 80/20 rule to focus on the critical tasks that will return the greatest benefit.

Amy, from the beginning of "Conserve Energy," used a shrink strategy in two ways: she shrank our sixty-minute coaching session to thirty minutes, and she shrank her reporting project down to a smaller deliverable so she could meet that personal commitment. Rebecca, in "Know What to Ignore," learned that she could meet people partway in their requests for her time. Lily shrunk her business development goals down to one SMART goal. Remember Amir, from way back at beginning of the book, who wished for more mentoring? He found small opportunities to capitalize upon. Shorter blocks of time are better. You have more focus and more energy and can deliver most of what people want from you.

Shrink It

Instead of giving up your schedule entirely and spending as much time as someone wants to take from you, shrink what time you can spend to how much time you have. You can still give them attention, show up, and do things. Just moderate and learn to negotiate how much time you commit. One move, three benefits: 1. you've set a future expectation that your time is precious and valuable (in other words, you'll have this conversation again, so lay the groundwork now); 2. you set a limit on what you can do and protected your important priorities; and 3. you haven't said no, but you've modified your yes. When you shrink to fit a task to your availability, you succeed in making a deposit with others and yourself.

How does this translate to your workday? First, look at how long you have available for tasks and work within that. Or, if you don't have time or other parameters, create some to help you optimize for maximum impact. Here's some examples:

- Shrink an hour meeting to fifteen minutes (you'll be amazed at how much you'll cover in so little time).
- Shrink time in email to quickly skimming for anything urgent and important and closing it rather than keeping it open all day.
- Shrink your involvement in a project to quick progress reviews and comments rather than being in the loop on everything.
- Shrink the number of design options down to two rather than the four you'd really like to do.
- Shrink your email response down to one sentence rather than a 300-word diatribe explaining every aspect of your thinking.
- Shrink that happy hour drink with a colleague down to walking together at lunch.
- Shrink the two-hour on-site client meeting to a forty-five-minute phone call.

The Fifteen-Minute Challenge

Alan Greenspan, former chair of the Federal Reserve, had good reason to be distracted by demands on his time, and he understood the value of focused time. He was known to adhere to the habit of working in fifteen-minute increments. Not splitting his attention on three things during those fifteen minutes. Focusing on one thing for fifteen minutes at a time. If you don't think your schedule allows big blocks of time, think in smaller increments.

Try turning off your phone and email, ask not to be bothered or work from home, and set your timer and focus on a single task for fifteen minutes. How do you feel about the quality of the work you did when you concentrated on just that? Fifteen minutes for email. Fifteen minutes for a meeting. Fifteen minutes on a proposal.

What if you approached your day in fifteen-minute blocks?

When other people try to interrupt you, apply the fifteen-minute rule: "I'm in the middle of something and just need fifteen minutes." After a while, they'll get the idea. Even with a plan and maintaining healthy boundaries on your time, things happen. Tasks take longer than you planned. People with clout demand your time. Conversations take longer. Try stopping and thinking throughout the day, how can I best use the next fifteen minutes? I love the simplicity and practicality of this approach.

⦿ Try It

1. Go into your calendar and look at your meetings. Which ones can you shrink?

2. Use triage mode in email more often. Pretend you're in a workshop and the instructor has given you a one-minute break to check your phone; then get back to work.

3. Answer emails like you're texting someone. Make it as brief as possible without information overload.

4. Practice preparing for debriefs by thinking about what the person really needs to know and what do you need from this person.

5. Schedule ten-minute standing meetings with your team to simply compare daily priorities and conflicts so you meet your commitments.

SHRINK TO WHAT WORKS
⌐···o GET IT DONE

Don't let perfect be the enemy of good.

VOLTAIRE

I once coached a PM and the VP, together, in the estimating division of a national general commercial contractor. Estimating is just that: giving your best guess on how much it will cost and how long it will take to build a project. The PM was meticulous in his estimates, often going over time to get it right. Clients loved him and appreciated his work (a deposit), but things rarely go as planned in construction. That's why they call it an estimate.

His VP answered directly to the CEO and was charged with making sure all projects moved along so they could get built, clients were happy, construction crews stayed busy, and the firm made money. He was in his position because he knew that a get it-right approach wasn't sustainable. It was just too expensive and robbed time from other projects to spend an inordinate amount of time on projects. He believed work had to be done right, but he had a get-it-done approach to projects, which translated to 85 percent correct instead of the PM's 98 percent standard. You can see where this discussion was headed.

The VP was frustrated that the PM held on to work so long, didn't delegate, and put in more time than was necessary on projects. Profitability on his projects suffered, his staff didn't grow, and the PM wasn't promoted to assist leading the department.

Worse yet, other clients were left waiting for work because the PM's hold on projects was a bottleneck. The PM's deposit of getting it right with his clients translated into multiple withdrawals when you think of all the people affected by the PM's singular focus on getting it right. Simply put, the PM had to shrink the amount of time he was spending on projects.

My first task was to get them to appreciate the other person's position. After all, there's merit in getting things done and moving along and merit in getting them done right. Appreciation is an important first step in a disagreement. Once there, the PM and VP had a language to begin negotiating.

After six months, the PM began to slowly back off his perfectionism. Instead of working ten hours on a project, he made himself shrink it to nine hours. The VP was still aiming for seven hours, but it was a step in the right direction.

O What They Learned

1. **Communication helps build trust and collaboration.**

2. **The world doesn't collapse when your grip loosens on a project.**

3. **Change is hard and can be slow to happen.**

Let Go Gradually

For the get-it-right doers, it will be challenging but important to discipline yourself to shrink a task to a budget of time. But like delegating, learning to economize how you're spending your time and working more efficiently is the only way to get to your mountain, not disappoint people, and actually have a life outside of work. Continue to hold on to projects and work until they're done right and see how well that works for you in the long run.

Experience is the best teacher in what's not that important to sweat the details. Start gradually, within your comfort level, to let

Shrink to What Works

1. Take Small Steps
2. Count Small Wins
3. Shrink to Fit
4. Get It Done

go of perfectionism. Seek out colleagues and mentors who are good at getting it done and also getting it right. Ask for their advice.

The shrink strategy is particularly powerful and useful. You don't have to think through as much as you do with the delegation and ignore strategies. Just start downsizing tasks and work in smaller increments.

Combine the DIS approach to time management to maintain your bank accounts, grow your team, and get you closer to your mountain, without running out of fuel.

O Try It

1. Find a task where the risk is very low if you take less time than you would typically take to complete it.

2. Watch the clock and work within a smaller time frame.

3. Leave it alone and let it go.

4. Observe if there were any consequences to shrinking the amount of time you spent on it.

5. Talk to a colleague or mentor to get advice on their philosophy and approach to operating between getting it right and getting it done.

STEP 4

the view from here

171   No More Chainsaws

179   Surprise Yourself

NO MORE CHAINSAWS

One of the most common causes of failure is the habit of quitting when one is overtaken by temporary defeat.

NAPOLEON HILL

In the beginning of this book, we met Pete, who questioned taking the leap into leadership. Did he have the right stuff to lead people and not just do the work? Would it mean a constant life of juggling chainsaws? Was it too much of a sacrifice?

Let's imagine Pete took every tool from this book. How would the story turn out if he did take the leap?

★ ★ ★

Pete's day starts the night before. He quickly checks his calendar to see what his schedule looks like, where he needs to be, and what he needs to do. He checks with his wife and compares schedules, so he doesn't make a careless withdrawal in any of his accounts from a lack of planning.

Pete stops checking emails shortly after dinner. He's off the clock and has informed clients and colleagues of his policy of when he's available and unavailable so that he can protect his free time with his family and have time to practice his guitar. He's stopped drinking alcohol so close to bedtime because it interferes with his sleep, which he needs for his busy days.

His alarm clock goes off at 6:00 a.m., which gives him enough time to relax with coffee on his deck, map out his day, and factor in any buffer time for unexpected emergencies, like pet accidents or sibling meltdowns. He takes a walk around his garden to see how the blueberries are doing or if the birds are taking more than their fair share.

He's already factored enough time to take his kids to school and get to his 9:00 a.m. meeting across town, even with the usual morning traffic. He's not stressed and instead uses the time to listen to an audio book on how Google builds productive teams. Because he checked his calendar the night before and he built in enough buffer time in the morning, he's had time to make sure he had the right address for the meeting, has the correct documents to review with the client, and was able to send a quick text to his team to remind them about the 10:20 morning huddle when he gets back into the office. As he texts, several new texts come through, but he decides to ignore them; it's more important to focus on his upcoming client meeting and getting there on time. So far, he's feeling good about meeting his commitments and maintaining his say-do ratio. No withdrawals.

When he gets to the client meeting at 9 a.m., no one is there. He uses the time to do some triage work answering texts and emails. When people start coming into the room at 9:10 a.m., he realizes this meeting is going to start twenty minutes late, which will derail his plan for meeting other commitments. This is more typical than uncommon. He feels himself get angry but read recently in *Emotional Intelligence 2.0* how to control and calm himself down when he gets triggered. He decides to shrink his commitment to his client and make a small withdrawal. When everyone finally arrives, Pete gently says, "I just need to let you know I have another commitment at ten, so I need to leave by ten at the latest. Can I present first?" Pete knows his account is full with this client, and it's not a significant withdrawal to leave at the time the client said it would end. Their inability to meet their own timelines wasn't going to cost Pete. He certainly could have justified going over time for the client's sake, but if he didn't establish a ground rule with the client, they would continue to start late and disrupt his schedule. If he didn't meet his schedule with staff, how could he keep them accountable to showing up on time and meeting any schedule? Better to make a strategic withdrawal now with the client and protect the rest of the day. Afterward, he texts his client to apologize for leaving before it was over, and the client says he understood. Before the next meeting he has with the client, Pete texts the client to confirm it will start and end as stated, because he again has a tight schedule. Everyone shows up on time.

When Pete does meet with his team for the huddle, he keeps it short and informs them of his schedule for the day, saying he needs uninterrupted time from 11:00 a.m. to 12:30 p.m. to write a proposal for a new project. He checks to see if a team member is able to proofread it this afternoon, so they can submit it by 4:00 p.m. Even though it is due at 5:00 p.m., it is important enough to factor in buffer time for anything that might come up.

Pete decides to take his laptop into the small conference room so he won't be interrupted. He puts a DO NOT DISTURB note on the door. Focusing on the proposal is important and time sensitive (urgent), everything else can wait. Sure enough, some people disregard the note. Shirley, from human resources, knocks on the door. "Sorry to disturb you, but I just need your signature on this vacation request from Tom." Pete pauses briefly and thinks, *I can do this because it will take five seconds.* But as soon as he is done, Shirley says, "Did you give any more thought on making an offer to the candidate for the estimator position?" Pete simply says, "Shirley, I need to get back to his proposal. Can we talk about this later? If I forget, please bug me. I know it's important." Shirley is agreeable and apologizes. Pete is temporarily off his focus and chooses to check his phone for any urgent and important texts or emails. After a quick scan, he sees there is nothing that requires an immediate response, so he gets back to work. Pete checks his watch at 12:20 p.m. He really needs to do more work on this proposal but has other commitments on his calendar.

Pete reaches out to his assistant, who knows his schedule from the morning huddle. Rather than reschedule meetings himself, he knows his time is better spent on writing the proposal. Pete asks his assistant to move some appointments and explain why it is important. While he is aware he is making small withdrawals with colleagues, he knows those meetings are not critical or time sensitive and can be moved. He does send off a few emails and texts to clients to make sure they are getting what they need. In terms of his bank accounts, Pete feels reasonably good about how he is handling his commitments and communicating with people.

He is aware that putting more time into the proposal is eating into critical review time for the staff person who is going to proofread it. He calls him to discuss the schedule, and they agree that he will send what he has done so far to get the proofreading going. The schedule will be a little tighter, but he is glad he has the buffer time in his schedule to accommodate the extra work required.

After passing off the proposal to the staff person, Pete calls his wife back, who left messages, to see how her day is going and what sounds good for dinner. She says she has to work late, and Pete offers to pick up pizza for the kids and have it waiting when she comes home. Pete looks at his schedule for the rest of the day, which got derailed with the proposal writing, and figures out what is the best use of the rest of the day. He spends time checking in on some work he delegated earlier in the week, making sure not to take the project over, but asks questions and encourages the staff person to keep working at it. They set another check-in time. Pete also decides to go out for coffee with his boss, Liz, instead of working on projects. He does a quick email to people and says he will reserve time in the morning to discuss developments on projects, and he'd appreciate it if people came with specific issues and their thoughts on how to solve them. He really wants to keep projects in people's courts and coach them by asking questions.

He is glad he meets with Liz. He learns there are some imminent changes in senior management. Liz also tells him that ownership has been impressed with how organized and productive Pete has been in his new position. She says not to be surprised if he gets tapped for a larger role. That might have freaked out Pete before, but he's more confident he can handle it. Despite the great conversation, Pete watches the time to make sure to get home and bring pizza, as he promised. "I'd love to continue this talk, but I have pizza duty tonight, so I have to run," Pete says. Liz smiles and says, "Understood." Before he leaves the office, Pete looks at his schedule for the next day and sets scheduled check-ins with his team on projects, as he said he would do. He sees that he has a morning meeting, which he isn't quite ready for.

After picking up pizza, he comes home to enjoy some time with his family. He tells them he has about an hour of work to do, and then he will make himself available for family game night. When he sees their looks, he says, "You know, I'll just get up early tomorrow to prepare. Let's have some fun!"

As he walks the dog later that night, he reflects on how things are going. He no longer feels stressed, like he is juggling chainsaws. He is excited about how well he is doing. By watching his emotional bank accounts and not forgetting about himself, he has become more conscious and intentional about capacity. He has learned to focus on what is truly important and become a leader others want to follow and the person he wanted to become.

★ ★ ★

The habits in this book will serve you not only in the next three years, but throughout your career. As you evolve as a leader, your mountains will change, but once you figure out how to conquer one mountain, your future potential is unlimited.

○ What Pete Learned— And What I Hope You've Learned

1. Take time to paint a picture of what's important to you in your life and career so you know where you're going.

2. Get the skills and experience any way you can; don't wait for an invitation.

3. You'll be more successful if your personal plan helps the company's goals.

4. Advocate for yourself; don't settle for what other people tell you.

5. Don't give up just because change is tough.

6. It's about relationships more than projects. Communication is key.

7. Make more deposits than withdrawals.

8. You need allies and support at many levels to be successful.

9. Meet your commitments and do what you say you'll do to build trust.

10. Be more aware that time is finite and be super aware of every minute.

11. Plan ahead to meet your commitments and get important work done.

12. Start your day slowly by establishing a schedule and meeting with your team to share priorities.

13. Make small, realistic goals that get you to your mountain.

14. Work in blocks—free, focus, reflection, and buffer—rather than multitasking.

15. Respectfully defend your boundaries rather than let people hijack your time.

16. Delegate, ignore, and shrink tasks and time sinks to stay on schedule.

17. Don't put yourself last. Protect your personal time.

18. Know what you can control and accept what you can't.

19. Celebrate and be grateful for any progress you make.

20. You never know how much you can surprise yourself if you don't try.

Try It

1. Examine your typical day by recounting how you started it, what choices you made, the nature of your interactions, and how well you maintained your say-do ratio.

2. What didn't go well that you want to stop doing?

3. What went well that you want to repeat?

4. What new strategy do you want to try?

5. Now redesign that day by scripting the way you want your tomorrow to go.

6. Repeat.

SURPRISE YOURSELF

My dad had Alzheimer's, and it was gut-wrenching to see him slip away. One year, I was visiting my parents during Christmas and to lighten the mood, my mother went to the piano and started playing "O Holy Night." I started singing as best I could, but this was really Dad's song. It had always been his favorite song. He had an incredibly resonant baritone and great range. His seven children would try to compete with him on the high notes, and he would soar far above us, leaving us croaking and falling off one by one. Just as I was psyching myself up to hit the crescendo, my father came up behind me and with full voice, sang, "Fall on your knees. . ." and finished the entire song. I was crying too much to join him. He couldn't remember who I was, but he could still recall the words to "O Holy Night."

Maybe all Alzheimer's patients have hidden creative talents that I could help untap, I wondered. After he died, I signed up to volunteer at an Alzheimer's center, working with residents on art therapy to honor him and help other patients find their inner muse. I couldn't have been more naïve. On my first day, I spent the entire time making sure the residents didn't wander off, answering the same question about which marker they should use, or encouraging them to do anything but stare down at their paper. At the end, defeated and drained, I felt like I had made a colossal mistake. When I was packing up the supplies, one resident hung back. Chuck, a white-haired, good-natured resident who still thought he was in World War II, looked down at his charming little sketch of a scruffy dog. I asked him if he had a good time today. He paused and said, "Yeah, I did. I surprised myself."

I'll never forget that moment because it woke me to realize we can't short-change anyone—especially ourselves. I went into the center with high expectations and was disappointed when they were not met. I learned that I couldn't help everyone, but I managed to help one person surprise himself and, in so doing, he surprised me.

You too have the capacity to surprise yourself and surprise others. You may realize through your journey that leadership truly isn't for you. That may be less of a surprise and more of a confirmation. If you're a supervisor, you probably can remember the many people you've tried to help change but with no effect. Maybe you don't think training and coaching will help. People are just who they are. A leopard doesn't change its spots, as the saying goes. It's true some people are more suited to be an individual contributor. But how often have you discovered your true capabilities only after a lot of hard work?

Do you really know what you are capable of if you haven't tried?

The emerging leaders I've portrayed in this book certainly questioned themselves. They didn't necessarily see themselves as natural leaders. They had doubts about how effective they would be and how much others would follow them. In more than twenty-five years of coaching emerging leaders, I have been surprised by how far people can go and how quickly they can transform how they think and act—and how just as quickly others' perceptions of them change.

How can you surprise yourself today?

NOTES

Know What You Want (p.11)

Simon Sinek: www.simonsinek.com

Learn How to Get There (p.25)

Jack Zenger and Joe Folkman, "Key Insights from the Extraordinary Leader," 2017, https://zengerfolkman.com/wp-content/uploads/2019/05/White-Paper-Extraordinary-Leader-Insights-Excerpts-from-The-Extraordinary-Leader.pdf.

Travis Bradberry and Jean Graves, *Emotional Intelligence 2.0* (TalentSmart, 2009).

Daniel Goleman, *Emotional Intelligence* (Random House, 2005).

Invest in Relationships (p.53)

Christopher Dollard, "Invest in Your Relationship: The Emotional Bank Account," The Gottman Institute, September 13, 2017, https://www.gottman.com/blog/invest-relationship-emotional-bank-account/.

Employee Engagement Study. Employee Job Satisfaction and Engagement Revitalizing a Changing Workforce, Society of Human Resources Management, 2015, https://www.shrm.org/hr-today/trends-and-forecasting/research-and-surveys/documents/2016-employee-job-satisfaction-and-engagement-report.pdf.

Delegate What You Can (p.77)

Cheryl Strayed, Wild: *From Lost to Found on the Pacific Coast Trail* (Vintage, 2012), is an inspirational read about self-discovery.

Liz Wiseman, *Multipliers: How the Best Leaders Make Everyone Smarter* (HarperBusiness, 2010). Quotes are from Wiseman's website about the book. The story about Henry Kissinger is also from the book. Excellent resource for new and senior managers alike. Excerpt: http://thewisemangroup.com/wp-content/uploads/2019/07/multipliers-chapter-1-the-multiplier-effect.pdf.

Curse of knowledge and commander's intent were gleaned from *Made to Stick* (Random House, 2007), by Dan Heath and Chip Heath, two of my favorite authors. Highly recommended. https://heathbrothers.com/.

William Oncken, Jr., and Donald L. Wass, "Management Time: Who's Got the Monkey?," *Harvard Business Review*, November–December 1999, https://hbr.org/1999/11/management-time-whos-got-the-monkey.

Daniel Pink, Drive: *The Surprising Truth About What Motivates Us* (Riverhead Books, 2011). Anything by Pink is worth reading www.danpink.com.

Brené Brown podcast on vulnerability. More at https://brenebrown.com/podcasts/.

Ignore The Unimportant (p.117)

Stephen Covey, *The 7 Habits of Highly Effective People*. Whatever the edition, it's a timeless classic on the fundamentals of what it takes to be a leader.

George Shultz's time management habits are cited by many authors, including this 1997 *New York Times* article by David Leonhardt, "You're Too Busy. You Need a Shultz Hour," https://www.nytimes.com/2017/04/18/opinion/youre-too-busy-you-need-a-shultz-hour.html.

Melissa Gratias on multitasking: Alia Hoyt, "How Multitasking Works," HowStuffWorks.com, https://science.howstuffworks.com/life/inside-the-mind/human-brain/multitasking.htm.

Shrink To What Works (p.147)

SMART goals: George Doran, Arthur Miller, and James Cunningham, "There's a S.M.A.R.T. Way to Write Management's Goals and Objectives," *Management Review*, November 1981.

Minding the Gap: Derived from a great program for entrepreneurs, Strategic Coach. Also from Strategic Coach, the question to define your mountain three years from now.

Alan Greenspan and Stephanie Vozza, "Why the Most Productive People Do These Six Things Every Day," *Fast Company*, January 13, 2017, https://www.fastcompany.com/3066982/why-the-most-productive-people-do-these-six-things-every-day.

ABOUT THE AUTHOR

Leo MacLeod, founder of **Training. Coaching. Pie.**, helps Architecture/Engineering/Construction (AEC) firms with coaching, training, and leadership transition. He regularly presents for the American Council of Engineering Companies and helped develop the Oregon chapter's popular leadership program. Leo speaks nationally on leadership development, emotional intelligence, and why baking pie is a great way to develop soft skills.

With a BA in English with honors from Portland State University, he's had a successful career as a freelance writer, fundraiser, and advertising executive and consultant. For many years, Leo has written columns for *Zweig Letter*, *Daily Journal of Commerce*, and *The Business Journal*.

He lives in Portland, Oregon, with his wife, Lisa, and spends his free time making pies and writing songs on his ukulele.

FIELD NOTES

1. What does career and personal life look like three
   years from now?

   _____
   _____
   _____
   _____

2. What's at the end that's worth the extra work?

   _____
   _____
   _____
   _____

3. What skills and knowledge do you need to get to
   your mountain?

   _____
   _____
   _____
   _____

4. How can you start moving toward your mountain today?

_____

_____

_____

_____

5. What tasks are weighing you down that you really shouldn't do?

_____

_____

_____

_____

6. How can you do the best job within the amount of time you have?

_____

_____

_____

_____

7. How can you surprise yourself today?

_____

_____

_____

_____

ONE FINAL NOTE

Dear Reader,

I took the most important lessons in this book and created **Pocket Tools**™, an online tool kit with 5-minute videos, discussion guides, and quizzes. Try a free preview of Pocket Tools™ by visiting **leomacleod.com/pocket-tools/**.

My website features blog posts and articles with practical advice for leaders at any level. And don't forget to subscribe to my newsletter to receive my **Ten Steps to Getting Your Time Back** download.

If you're interested in group leadership training, contact me directly at **leo@leomacleod.com**.

www.ingramcontent.com/pod-product-compliance
Lightning Source LLC
Chambersburg PA
CBHW030510210326
41597CB00013B/859